The Fall of
KHRUSHCHEV

THE FALL OF
KHRUSHCHEV

William Hyland and
Richard Wallace Shryock

FUNK & WAGNALLS New York

To my Mother, and to Lynn, Billy, and Jimmy

W.H.

To my Father, Richard Harrison Shryock

R.W.S.

■ Contents

▪ Prologue

When Josef Stalin died in March 1953, few in the West could have guessed that Nikita Sergeyevich Khrushchev would one day be the man to challenge and defeat all other claimants to the old dictator's mantle. Khrushchev was not well known to the outside world; he was a stocky, faintly comical little man with a peasant face and little to distinguish him from the scores of party apparatchiki who had surrounded Stalin. Yet he had been, in fact, a member of Stalin's inner circle for years, and if the world at large could not know of his considerable talents, his colleagues were surely aware of them and, indeed, would soon have reason to regret them.

Those who initially overshadowed Khrushchev did not do so for long. Khrushchev joined in the successful move to destroy the sinister secret-police chief, Lavrenti Beria, in June 1953. In 1955 he elbowed Stalin's nominal heir, Georgi Malenkov, into the rear ranks and humiliated the old Bolshevik, Vyacheslav Molotov, into a confession of error. And at the Geneva summit conference in 1955 he pushed Premier Nikolai Bulganin out of the limelight and revealed himself to President Eisenhower as the real power in the Soviet delegation. But it was his famous speech denouncing Stalin in early 1956 which signaled Khrushchev's all-out drive for unchallenged leadership, and from that time forward Khrushchev's career was to be intimately intertwined with the posthumous fortunes of his predecessor.

Khrushchev's greatest moment may have come in June 1957 when he finally succeeded in completely crushing his opponents, despite their ability to muster a majority against him in the party's top body, the Presidium. Indeed, the Khrushchev era may be dated from that point. There followed his consolidation of power—a process which required the taming of the military, principally through the firing of the renowned Marshal Georgi Zhukov—and the forceful entry of the Soviet Union into international politics on a global scale. Flushed with the success of Sputnik in 1957 and an unusually bountiful harvest in 1958, Khrushchev challenged the West in Berlin, rattled his intercontinental rockets in the Middle East, and reached out to involve his country in far-off places and exotic circumstances—in the Congo, in Indonesia, in Cuba. He risked tearing up his alliance with Mao Tse-tung and splitting the Communist world into two warring camps. He called for coexistence with the United States and visited Washington and Camp David to declare peace. And later, in another mood, he traveled to New York to embrace Castro and to pound his shoe at the United Nations. But, finally, in his frustration, in his desperation at his failure to produce a world triumph—one which would, among other things, dispel a gathering political storm at home—he resorted to his greatest gamble and brought the world to the brink of nuclear war in Cuba.

The outcome of that crisis was defeat abroad—including the Soviet Union's mortifying withdrawal of weapons at the demand of its prime international adversary—and, for Khrushchev, a grave weakening of his position at home—

involving a self-abasing retreat on the issue of de-Stalinization at the insistence of his major domestic opponents. From
Cuba onward, in fact, Khrushchev was largely on the defensive. Ultimately, of course, his ramparts were broken
and, swiftly and without open protest, he was torn from the
political scene.

Surprisingly, though, Khrushchev is still somewhat with
us. He even continues quietly to exercise his franchise. Wear-
ing that squarely-set Russian derby and a weak smile, he
made a rare appearance not long ago in Moscow on his way
to the polling station—the one, ironically enough, patronized
by his old enemy Molotov. He also made an appearance on
American television last year. He looked tired, defeated,
building little bonfires to pass the time of day—a far cry
from the man who had once threatened to consume the
world in flames.

Khrushchev turned 74 in April, 1968. Any hope he may
once have had of returning to politics is surely gone. He
now has only his memories of high privilege and power, and
these must be, at best, a mixed blessing. He no doubt feels,
at a minimum, that his job was unfinished when he was
forced from office. At worst, he might believe in his own
consummate failure as a Soviet leader. One of his content-
ments, however, must be that those who have followed him
—a more cautious and less colorful lot—have as yet to prove
that they can succeed where he had failed.

The Fall of
KHRUSHCHEV

1. The Setting

THE FALL OF NIKITA KHRUSHCHEV came as a shock. The old man had weathered monumental crises—the challenge of Molotov and Malenkov, the U-2 affair, the Cuban missile fiasco—and in the autumn of 1964 he appeared to be in fine fettle. Most of the close observers of the mysteries of Kremlin politics had pronounced him safe.[1] But suddenly he was gone, the object of a cryptic and dishonest communiqué:

> The plenum of the Central Committee satisfied the request of N. S. Khrushchev to relieve him of the duties of First Secretary of the Central Committee, member of the Presidium of the Central Committee, and Chairman of the Council of Ministers U.S.S.R. in connection with advanced age and poor health.[2]

It may well be that the final story of Khrushchev's fall—including the details of the intricate and dangerous plotting that must have preceded the coup—will forever remain among the great secrets of Soviet politics. Certainly the present close-mouthed Soviet leadership is unlikely to sponsor a "secret speech" concerning Khrushchev akin to Khrushchev's famous exposé of Stalin in 1956. It is possible, nevertheless, to reconstruct the day-to-day sequence of events which attended his final defeat and to trace, as the necessary preliminaries to those events, the decline of his fortunes in the last years of his reign.

The story really begins in late 1961. Khrushchev, though by no means an easy man to dismay, at that time probably contemplated the future with some considerable uneasiness. He faced, in fact, a generally bleak outlook both at home and abroad, and there is reason to believe, especially on the basis of his subsequent behavior and policies, that he was quite conscious of this. And even if not completely discouraged about his prospects, Khrushchev was certainly well aware of the rather dismal record of the recent past.

Indeed, by 1960 and 1961 the U.S.S.R.'s major foreign policies were in deep trouble. Khrushchev had rested his plans and his hopes on three fairly simple propositions. In the first full flush of impressive post-Stalin economic gains on the home front, the orbiting of the sensational Sputnik I, and the first successful tests of intercontinental rockets, he had assumed, and so stated in 1957 and 1958, that the balance of power between East and West would soon fundamentally change in the U.S.S.R.'s favor. With this expectation in mind, he had decided to press an offensive against the West, confident in his second assumption that the Communist camp would remain a cohesive political entity on the basis of the new unity achieved in the wake of the Hungarian disaster. Finally, he had assumed that, in the Third World, the breakup of the colonial system would inevitably provide opportunities to expand greatly the power and influence of the Soviet Union at Western expense. Within a few years all of these assumptions had either been placed in grave doubt or had been exposed as manifestly in error.

The United States, though for a time overawed by Sputnik and overpersuaded by Moscow's boasts of a missile gap, had not changed its behavior because of the image of Soviet strategic superiority. By early 1962, it was fast becoming apparent that this image had been false and that—as Moscow no doubt feared—the world would soon recognize the reality of American strategic preponderance.[3] Moreover, the United States and its allies in Western Europe, while hardly of one mind concerning their exposed position in West Berlin, had refused to be seduced by the "Spirit of Camp David" in 1960 or intimidated by the threat of nuclear extinction in 1961, and had yielded not at all on the issue of a German peace treaty.

It was no secret in late 1961 that Khrushchev's most glaring failure was in Berlin. He deliberately chose this city in 1958 as the test case for his conviction that the balance of world power had dramatically changed. But his search for a definitive political solution in Central Europe not only eluded him but drove him deeper and deeper into confrontation with the United States, a process which reverberated against his worldwide ambitions and his domestic objectives as well.

For a time in 1959 events still had seemed in some respects to be moving Khrushchev's way. He had retreated from his initial ultimatum of November 1958 demanding that West Berlin be transformed into a "free city" within six months, but he had also proved that Soviet pressures could bring the Western powers to the conference table in Geneva to talk about a question which they really did not wish to discuss, much less negotiate. But at the Geneva foreign ministers meeting in mid-1959, the East-West stalemate over basic issues began to emerge with greater clarity.

Khrushchev's visit to the United States in 1959 provided a colorful interlude and triumph of sorts (though it must have been a final irony for Khrushchev to learn that the visit came

about through a mixup in the Eisenhower Administration).
In effect, however, Khrushchev, by committing the U.S.S.R.
to a successful outcome of a summit meeting in Paris, mort-
gaged his policy to the good intentions of Dwight D. Eisenhower. Only if the scheduled summit yielded significant
gains on Berlin could Khrushchev justify his withdrawal of
the "free city" ultimatum and his large investment in the
"Spirit of Camp David." And then, in the spring of 1960, on
the eve of the Paris conference with Eisenhower, Charles De
Gaulle, and Harold Macmillan, came the U-2 incident.
Khrushchev characteristically tried to exploit the incident
and put the U.S. on the defensive when the conference
opened. But he carefully allowed the President an opening
to claim ignorance of the entire affair. The President's startling assumption of personal responsibility for the overflights
of the Soviet Union stunned Khrushchev; he was humiliated
and had no choice but to break up the Paris meeting in a
towering rage. After eighteen months of campaigning on the
Berlin issue he was back where he had started, glowering at
the West, only hoping that a change of American administrations would bring new opportunities.

An opportunity, of course, did come. In June 1961,
Khrushchev faced another American president, this time in
Vienna. As President John F. Kennedy later remarked, most
of his talks with Khrushchev were over Berlin.[4] The personnel had changed but not the issues and not the impasse.
Once again the crisis began, and this time it led to the infa-
mous Berlin Wall. In later years Khrushchev was to praise
the Wall as a major triumph, and it was at least something to
show for his efforts; the paroxysm of East German refugees
was at last abated. But it was humiliating to admit that the
very state he put forward as the basis for a unified Germany
was in fact a virtual prison. Moreover, the Wall was the only
trophy he could display after three years of intensive efforts

to force the West into recognizing his demands for a final postwar settlement in Central Europe. And perhaps worst of all, the forms and the failures of his Western policies had played into the hands of his principal adversary in the East, Mao Tse-tung, who had vigorously argued against Khrushchev's effort to gain his objectives through rapprochement.

The theoretical, historical, and political bases and motives shaping the Sino-Soviet conflict have been thoroughly explored and need not be repeated here.[5] It is enough to say that by the time Khrushchev returned to Moscow from the United States, via Peking, there were serious problems. There is now good reason to believe that in 1959 Khrushchev had reneged on an obligation to give China a "sample" atom bomb; that he had proposed unacceptable military conditions to the Sino-Soviet partnership; and that he had involved himself in internal Chinese politics, backing the loser in a struggle between Mao and Marshal Peng Teh-huai.[6] But to make matters worse Khrushchev had gone to the United States, proclaimed far and wide the theme of "peaceful coexistence," and then traveled to Peking where he publicly warned Mao against "testing" the capitalist system by force.[7]

Khrushchev's detente with Eisenhower was anathema to Mao, who was inclined to see the Soviet peace offensive as an abandonment of Communist principles and, worse, an abandonment of Communist China. Mao privately made his views known to Khrushchev when the latter was in Peking, and gradually the fundamental disagreement over worldwide strategy began to emerge. In April 1960, for example, the Chinese summed up their reservations in a series of articles in party publications, thus in effect surfacing the dispute in public.[8] After the U-2 incident and the collapse of the Paris summit conference in May—a development which seemed to substantiate the Chinese case—Peking pressed anew for a basic change in the Soviet line, but to no avail. Indeed, with his Western policy frozen until Eisenhower left office, Khrushchev turned his attention to the growing challenge of the Chinese.

At the Rumanian party Congress in June 1960, Khrushchev launched a surprise attack. He publicly demanded, in effect, that the Chinese cease their factional activities and submit to Soviet leadership. When this failed to shake the Chinese, he resorted to extreme measures: within a month he began the complete withdrawal of Russian technicians and experts from China.[9] The result was an economic disaster of the first magnitude for the Chinese, already in deep trouble because of Mao's Great Leap Forward. But, again, Khrushchev failed to intimidate the Chinese. A paper compromise in October-November 1960 provided a brief respite, but it was now apparent to the Soviets and Chinese that they were locked in a life and death struggle. The centralized world Communist movement was breaking apart, and another of Khrushchev's fundamental assumptions—that there could be no real divergence between Soviet interests and those of other Communist states and parties—was being shattered.

Compounding the U.S.S.R's problems with the West and with China was a general change in the world situation which Khrushchev had not foreseen. There was beginning to be discernible in the rest of the world a far more uneven and chaotic situation than Khrushchev had ever outlined in his various pronouncements. The U.S.S.R. suffered a serious setback in late 1959 in Iraq, when Moscow's good friend, Premier Abdul Kassem, slaughtered Iraqi Communists by the hundreds.[10] A dispute erupted with President Gamal Abdel Nasser during the same year, and this took some time to resolve.[11] At the same time, Khrushchev was finding it more and more difficult to reconcile his friendly overtures to De

Gaulle with his support for the Algerian rebels. And, in all of these instances, the Chinese were noisily seeking to exploit Soviet embarrassment.

Perhaps most important in this period was the U.S.S.R.'s stinging defeat in the Congo in 1960. Khrushchev had leaped into this chaotic mess in July to support the forces of Patrice Lumumba and Antoine Gizenga. Events seemed to be moving well for the Soviet position when Khrushchev for some strange reason agreed to intervention by the United Nations.[12] Almost immediately, however, he regretted it and began a campaign of denunciation of the UN's operations and its Secretary General, Dag Hammarskjold. Khrushchev also reverted to vague threats of Soviet military intervention in the Congo and, in fact, the U.S.S.R. supplied material to the Lumumba forces. But Soviet aspirations began to evaporate; the General Assembly voted overwhelmingly in favor of a resolution calling on all states to supply aid only through the UN. This was a direct slap at Khrushchev and preceded his arrival in New York by only a few days. In reaction, Khrushchev staged his famous shoe-pounding spectacle and launched his troika scheme to revamp the administrative structure of the UN executive arm.

The U.S.S.R. emerged from the Congo crisis in a weakened position; it had been defeated on an important issue of prestige and now was isolated within the UN. The reasons for its isolation were not that Moscow had supported Lumumba or had failed to support the revolutionary side, as claimed by China, but rather that, after this episode, many Africans believed that the U.S.S.R. had simply been playing the game of power politics with an essentially African issue.

In sum, concerning Soviet foreign policy during these years, the U.S.S.R. had lost much of its momentum, and there appeared to be little on the horizon, other than possibly Cuba, likely to restore it. Perhaps this bleak picture is what Khrushchev had in· the back of his mind when he reminded the 22nd Soviet Communist Party Congress in October 1961 that "history does not develop in a straight line—it makes gigantic bends, zigzags, and turns." [13] In any event, nothing seemed to illustrate the general stagnation of Soviet foreign policy at the time better than the two principal foreign policy declarations of that same Congress, *viz.* the graceless withdrawal of the second Soviet ultimatum on Berlin, and the bizarre, and impotent, denunciations of Communist China's sole ally in Europe, miniscule Albania.[14]

If Khrushchev thus seemed to face mainly frustration abroad, it would have been natural to seek some form of economic or political solace at home. But matters here were hardly more encouraging. Indeed, Khrushchev's lack of tangible domestic accomplishment since roughly 1958 was coming more and more to threaten both the substance of his programs and the stability of his position.

By early 1962, Khrushchev's campaign to reshape the economy and to alter its allocational priorities—central to so much of what he wished to do—was falling far short of its goals, and even Khrushchev himself, in trying to press the campaign forward, showed signs of faltering.[15] His various schemes for rationalizing the nation's economic structure, through major administrative overhauls and minor doctrinal adjustments, were meeting with indifferent success or were simply adding to the general confusion and inefficiency. The economy itself was beginning to grind into the slowdown so evident in later years. In the all-important agricultural sector, output had in effect leveled off since 1958 and, on a per capita basis, had actually declined. This, not surprisingly in view of his own promises and expectations, seemed to produce in Khrushchev a feeling akin to desperation.[16]

Adverse foreign developments were contributing to

Khrushchev's internal economic and political difficulties. Behind Khrushchev's grand design for domestic growth and for
economic competition with the West lay a presumption of
relative tranquility on the world scene, a tranquility which
somehow was supposed to survive even vigorous Soviet moves
against the West. Clearly, in the words of one Western observer, the capital investment program laid out in Khrushchev's Seven-Year Plan for 1960–1965 would require "maxi-
mal mobilization of the nation's resources." Thus, "any
worsening of international relations that would require in-
creased defense spending would threaten the program." [17]

When international relations did indeed worsen following
the U-2 incident in 1960 and the revival of tension over Berlin in 1961, Khrushchev's programs unquestionably suffered
as a result. The sizeable reduction in the troop strength of
the armed forces, which Khrushchev had announced after
his visit to the U.S., was suspended in mid-1961, the defense
budget was raised, and general economic plans—especially
those designed to boost living standards and de-emphasize
investment in heavy industry—were adjusted accordingly.[18]

Khrushchev's position was by no means so secure that he
could afford to overlook the political consequences of such
domestic and foreign setbacks. Indeed, from roughly the
time of the U-2 incident onward, Khrushchev seems to have
been confronted with an increasingly effective opposition.[19]
This stemmed from the ambition of his fellow politicians,
their contempt for his style of leadership, and their alarm
over his efforts to create his own ominous "cult of personality." It was also the result of real concern over his radical
ideas and "adventurist" policies among the defenders of ideological purity and, more important, among the members of
various vested interest groups, such as the military.

The opposition to Khrushchev took many forms and origi-
nated in diverse quarters, but found its most meaningful ex-

pression in the high organs of the party, particularly within the top governing body, the Presidium of the Central Committee (the successor to the old Politburo). The dozen or so members of the Presidium, charged with the day-to-day formulation of party (and thus national) policy, were in theory co-equals. In fact, of course, some were considerably more powerful than others, and Khrushchev was the most powerful of them all. Indeed, the Soviet press often referred to the Presidium as an organ with Khrushchev "at its head," though, in fact, there was no statutory provision whatsoever for any such distinction.

Resistance to Khrushchev sometimes broke through the surface and became evident in Soviet publications. To a great extent, of course, Khrushchev dominated the central press. Not only did he sit at the apex of the party's mechanism for press control, he also appointed many of the key editors: *e.g.*, his son-in-law, Alexei Adzhubei, editor of the government paper *Izvestia*, and Pavel Satyukov, editor of the party organ *Pravda* (both of whom were immediately dismissed in the wake of Khrushchev's fall). Nevertheless, the other leaders were not completely foreclosed from at least esoteric forms of public dissent. Usually this appeared in speeches, which the papers were more or less obligated to publish. Sometimes it appeared in articles in specialized journals or in the provincial press. Much of the debate over Khrushchev's military policy, for example, was carried on in various military magazines under the guise of comments on the Soviet Army's performance in World War II. On rare occasions, a challenge to some aspect or other of Khrushchev's policy would be more direct; a Presidium member, for example, might pointedly ignore a favorite theme of the First Secretary's, or he might emphasize his views in such a way as to contradict Khrushchev's preferences. Finally, the various media would reflect disagreement at the top and a possible weakening of Khrushchev's position by their failure to provide coverage of certain important but controversial policy questions, or by their seemingly inexplicable abandonment of publicity campaigns initiated by Khrushchev.

Thus, while Khrushchev was clearly preeminent, he was by no means another Stalin and could not afford to suppress or ignore the opinions and the powers of his senior colleagues. At least half of the Presidium members had had long and, in a sense, distinguished party careers of their own; they were not, in other words, simply creatures of Khrushchev's. Some of these leaders had their own followers and allies, men whose first loyalties did not lie with Khrushchev. And some had, or sought, the backing of important interests—the military, the heavy industry "lobby," the government bureaucrats—within the establishment. As "head" of the Presidium, as First Secretary of the party (charged with the implementation of policy), and as Prime Minister of the U.S.S.R., Khrushchev was almost always the initiator of policy. But he was not immune to the pressures and vagaries of politics at the top, nor could he avoid the constraints at times imposed on him by his comrades, especially in the aggregate.

It was a rare occasion, of course, when the Presidium members acted in concert in opposition to Khrushchev. But the Presidium did vote on questions of major importance (and some minor ones as well), and there is no doubt that these votes sometimes did not go Khrushchev's way. The decision of a majority of the Presidium to force Khrushchev out of office in June 1957—the action of the so-called anti-party group of Malenkov and Molotov which was subsequently overruled by the Central Committee—was, for example, one such occasion. And there were several others. According to a credible story, the Presidium met and voted in 1960 to let Khrushchev go to the summit in Paris, but it also decided to deny him the choice of whether to proceed with negotiations in the event that President Eisenhower failed to apologize for the U-2 incident.[20]

The long struggle of Khrushchev to have his opponents of the anti-party group expelled from the party and possibly subjected to legal punishment seems to have run into consistent (and for many years successful) opposition from the Presidium. Unresolved economic questions faced by the leadership over the years also suggested unfavorable Presidium reactions to some of Khrushchev's proposals. The question of industrial priorities—light vs. heavy industry, consumer vs. producers goods—remained at issue long after Khrushchev had clearly indicated his desire to reverse the unfavorable ratio for the consuming public. The forceful, sometimes devious, means Khrushchev used to gain his way in this dispute were only partially successful and the matter was by no means settled before his removal.

Various devices used by Khrushchev over the years testify in themselves to the lack of high-level consensus on various issues, to the apparent fact that Khrushchev could expect in some instances to face strong opposition to his innovations. His efforts to dilute the power of the Central Committee by packing its sessions with experts who were not members, and his proclivity, for which he was later chastised, for announcing the agenda of a Central Committee meeting prior to its convocation clearly represented efforts to outplay or overwhelm the opposition.

Soviet politics were not, of course, confined to formal sessions of the Presidium (which usually were called about once a week). Between sessions of the Presidium there was a great deal of contact and discussion between members. This, among other things, gave Khrushchev an opportunity to lobby, persuade, wheedle, and intimidate in advance of his introduction of a subject for discussion. It also offered him a chance to size up the opposition, if any, and he almost certainly delayed or canceled the introduction of some issues to the body as a whole when he discovered majority sentiment against him. Sometimes, when faced with this sort of problem, he would take his case "to the people" and then to the Central Committee in an effort to bypass the Presidium.

One great advantage enjoyed by Khrushchev was that the size and composition of the opposition would vary with the issue. Khrushchev's friend and colleague, Anastas Mikoyan, for example, could be counted on to support his chief's pro-consumer policies but not to go along with his efforts to punish the anti-party group. Eminent Presidium member Mikhail Suslov balked at Khrushchev's proposals for abolishing the machine tractor stations in 1958, but almost certainly went along with the First Secretary's doctrinal ripostes to the Chinese. Another top Presidium member, Frol Kozlov, won the respect of his boss by demonstrating his talents as a party organizer and manager, but—if for a time a close ally of Khrushchev's within the party—he later came to distrust Khrushchev's too-lenient cultural policies and to dislike Khrushchev's de-emphasis of heavy industry.

Members of the Presidium could come to resist Khrushchev on matters of foreign policy as well. Indeed, these same three men—Mikoyan, Suslov, and Kozlov—are all portrayed by Oleg Penkovsky (the Soviet official who spied for the British and the Americans) as, at best, unhappy about Khrushchev's tough line on Berlin in 1961. Penkovsky claims that in this they were not alone; the Soviet military establishment was also concerned, particularly about the possible consequences of a crisis over Berlin in which the U.S.S.R., in no position to confront the United States militarily, might be forced to the very brink.[21]

As time went on, individual high-level politicians in the U.S.S.R. who had problems with Khrushchev's policies also found themselves increasingly frustrated by Khrushchev's disinclination to share power. Some, probably including Miko-yan, were willing to live with this problem or were at least unwilling to seek real change. Others, however, almost cer-tainly including Kozlov, were more ambitious than Mikoyan and, in addition, had reason to become more and more un-comfortable about their ability to survive Khrushchev's ruth-less penchant for political games and oneupmanship.[22]

Frol Kozlov was the man who in 1959 had been voted by Khrushchev as the most likely to succeed to the First Secre-taryship upon Khrushchev's death or retirement.[23] It was no secret in the Soviet party that the political mortality rate of heirs apparent—always potential rivals of the Number One —was quite high. And, indeed, in the spring of 1962, Kozlov seemed to suffer a strange political reversal, one which, moreover, had been engineered by Khrushchev himself. One of Kozlov's high-level protégés, Ivan Spiridonov, a candi-date member of the Presidium and the first secretary of the party organization in Leningrad (where Kozlov had been reared), had been promoted to full membership on the Pre-sidium at the 22nd Party Congress in October 1961. Simulta-neously, Andrei Kirilenko, the protégé of another senior member of the Presidium, Leonid Brezhnev, had been de-moted from the Presidium and sent out to the provinces. Suddenly, however, only some six months later, this process was reversed: Kozlov's colleague, Spiridonov, was dropped from the Presidium and then removed from his post in Len-ingrad, and Brezhnev's man, Kirilenko, resumed his duties on the Presidium. In a highly unusual move, which had the effect of directing the party's entire attention to the episode, Khrushchev made the journey to Leningrad to attend the local party meeting which fired Spiridonov. All of this, of course, at least hinted of severe problems ahead for Kozlov.

The picture that emerges from all this—the interplay of

politics, the opposition of Presidium members, the restraints imposed on Khrushchev, and the indirect moves by Khrushchev against his rivals—is, of course, that of an oligarchy at the apex of the Soviet hierarchy rather than simply one man. But this, in a sense, is misleading, for, if an oligarchy, it was one of a very special nature, dominated most of the time by its very strong and forceful chairman. To him belonged most of the reins of power which extended out from the Presidium. He could be convinced not to use those reins; he could even on occasion be enjoined from using them by a majority of his colleagues. But he was, clearly, more than merely "more equal" than the others.

Sometime in the early 1960s, however, Khrushchev must have begun to realize that, as dominant but not supreme, he was in danger of losing his preeminence, of some day becoming the victim of his own apparent inability to produce. No longer could he count on old ways and past triumphs to rescue him from present difficulties and looming failures; everything from the once Virgin Lands (which were no more, and looked it) to the Allies in West Berlin (who intended to remain there, and also looked it) had, in a sense, let him down. Khrushchev, standing at the brink of 1962, was in need of some new and dramatic means to demonstrate to his restive colleagues, to his unhappy constituents, and to a skeptical world at large that his genius, far from ebbing, had in fact persisted.

Apparently late in 1961 or early in 1962, the thought came to him, or to someone close to him, that an answer to many of his problems might be found in Cuba. Here, some 5,000 miles removed from the Communist homeland, was the site of a self-styled socialist revolution which, more and more found itself exposed to U.S. hostility and dependent on Soviet support. Khrushchev's understandable doubt as to the authenticity of Castro's socialist credentials perhaps had for a time blinded the First Secretary to the full Cuban potential. But then, faced with the real need, Khrushchev finally saw the opportunity facing him, seized it, and finally, characteristically, sought to make entirely too much of it.

NOTES

1. Richard Lowenthal, "Fortschritt und Reaktion in der Innenpolitik," *Ost Europa*, No. 9/10, 1964, p. 795.

2. *Pravda*, October 16, 1964.

3. Arnold Horelick, *The Cuban Missile Crisis*, The RAND Corporation, Memorandum RM 3779-PR, September 1963. Also see Arnold Horelick and Myron Rush, *Strategic Power and Soviet Foreign Policy*, The RAND Corporation, R-434-PR, August 1965, pp. 129–160, for a comprehensive discussion.

4. The American side of the Vienna meeting is presented by two of President Kennedy's close advisors, Theodore C. Sorensen, *Kennedy* (New York, 1966), and Arthur A. Schlesinger, *A Thousand Days* (Boston, 1965).

5. The most comprehensive treatments are Donald S. Zagoria, *The Sino-Soviet Conflict 1956–61* (Princeton, 1962), Richard Lowenthal, *World Communism* (New York, 1964), and *The Sino-Soviet Dispute*, G.F. Hudson (ed.), (New York, 1963).

6. The Chinese accusations against Khrushchev are found in *The Polemic on the General Line of the International Communist Movement* (Peking, Foreign Languages Press, 1965). Some more specific charges are included in William Griffith, *The.Sino-Soviet Conflict* (Cambridge, 1964), p. 351. Also see David A. Charles, "The Dismissal of Marshal Peng Teh-huai," *The China Quarterly*, No. 8, October-December 1961, p. 63. For the military aspects of the dispute see Raymond L. Garthoff, *Soviet Military Policy* (New York, 1966), pp. 180–181.

7. *Current Digest of the Soviet Press* (CDSP) Vol. XI, No. 39, October 28, 1959, p. 21.

8. *Long Live Leninism* (Peking, Foreign Languages Press, 1960).

9. Griffith, *The Sino-Soviet Conflict*, p. 402.

10. *The Mizan Newsletter*, No. 4, April 1959, London, pp.

5–8 and appendix, and *ibid.*, No. 11, November 1959, pp. 3–5.

11. *Ibid.*, No. 2, February 1959, pp. 3–9; also No. 3, March 1959, pp. 7–8.

12. Khrushchev's Congo policies are discussed in David Morrison, *The U.S.S.R. and Africa* (London, 1964). Also see the supplement to *Mizan Newsletter*, No. 7, July-August 1960, "Soviet Documents on the Congo," and subsequent issues of *Mizan Newsletter* for Soviet involvement in the Congo crisis.

13. Moscow Domestic Service, October 18,1961.

14. Khrushchev, in effect, withdrew his ultimatum to the Western powers by denying that one had ever existed: "Proposing to sign a German peace treaty, the Soviet government did not put forward any ultimatum, but was prompted by the necessity of finally solving this urgent question. . . ." (*Ibid.*) Concerning Albania, he told the Congress, *inter alia:* "It is now no secret that the Albanian leaders remain in power by resorting to violence and arbitrariness. . . . Surely even in the darkest days of reactionary violence, the Czar and his satraps who tortured revolutionaries did not dare [as did the Albanian leaders] to execute pregnant women!" (Moscow, TASS, October 28, 1961.)

15. Signs during the spring of 1961 that Khrushchev was prepared to push hard for his consumer-oriented programs had faded by fall, and in October he presented to the 22nd Congress production targets which placed renewed emphasis on heavy industry. See Harry Schwartz, *The Soviet Economy Since Stalin* (Philadelphia, 1965), pp. 126, 127; also Sidney Ploss, *Conflict and Decision-Making in Soviet Russia* (Princeton, 1965), pp. 234–239.

16. "As 1961 closed, the Soviet leadership was faced by the hard fact that [after three years of the Seven-Year Plan] . . . almost no progress had been made toward reaching . . . farm goals. Something like panic seems to have seized Premier Khrushchev. He clearly cast about for some expedient . . . [which would] improve farm output in 1962, regardless of long-term consequences. . . ." (Schwartz, p. 163.) And Khrushchev himself, speaking in March 1962, revealed the depth of his dis-

tress and the magnitude of the problem: "We have been striving for forty years to attain the present level of [agricultural] production. Now we must do twice or three times as much and not in forty years but in just a few. . . . If we do not fulfill this task, the country will face great difficulties and serious harm will be inflicted on the cause of building communism." (Speech to Central Committee Plenum, March 5, 1962.)

17. Schwartz, p. 134.

18. Khrushchev announced the troop cut on January 14, 1960, in the midst of the "Spirit of Camp David," and linked the move in this and subsequent speeches to his efforts to boost living standards. Less than two years later he was forced to retract: "The Soviet Government," he told the 22nd Party Congress, "was forced [to halt the reduction of armed forces planned for 1961], to increase defense appropriations . . . and to resume nuclear tests. . . ." (Moscow Domestic Service, October 18, 1961.)

19. See Carl Linden, *Khrushchev and the Soviet Leadership 1957–1964* (Baltimore, 1966), pp. 90–108; also Ploss, pp. 184, 191.

20. Chalmers Roberts, *Washington Post*, June 12, 1960.

21. Oleg Penkovsky, *Penkovsky Papers* (New York, 1965) pp. 207–09, 216.

22. For a good account of military opposition to Khrushchev during this period, see Matthew P. Gallagher, "Military Manpower: A Case Study," *Problems of Communism*, XIII, May-June 1964, pp. 53–56. For discussions of the political and economic opposition, see Ploss, 184–252; Linden, *Khrushchev and the Soviet Leadership*, pp. 72–145; Linden, "Khrushchev and the Party Battle," *Problems of Communism*, XII, September-October 1963, pp. 27–31; Robert Conquest, "After the Fall: Some Lessons," *Problems of Communism*, XIV, January-February 1965, pp. 17–22; and (for underlying economic factors) Schwartz, pp. 121–128, 144, 160–164.

23. Khrushchev indicated to W. Averell Harriman in Moscow in June 1959 that Kozlov was his likely successor. See *The New York Times*, July 2, 1959, p. 1. Kozlov's number two posi-

tion in the hierarchy was confirmed at the 22nd Party Congress in October 1961 when Kozlov was listed out of alphabetical order as the second man on the Central Committee Secretariat, *i.e.* immediately after Khrushchev. See *The New York Times,* November 1, 1961, pp. 1, 4.

2. The Origins of Crisis

GENERAL EISENHOWER RELATES in his memoirs that his Administration spent considerable time and energy in early 1959 debating whether Fidel Castro was a real Communist, a crypto-pseudo-neo-Communist, or merely a naive politician.[1] The final conclusion seems to have been that, if Castro had not been a Communist on January 1, 1959, he was at least well on his way. There was a certain irony in this, if only because the Soviets themselves were from the start highly dubious about Castro's Marxist-Leninist credentials. Khrushchev and Castro performed an intricate minuet for almost three years before finally embracing each other within the socialist camp.

The Soviets, of course, knew a lot about Castro, but what they knew they did not especially like. At least this is the impression conveyed by the Soviets' cool treatment of Castro's revolution in its early days and by the activities and statements of Soviet-oriented Cuban Communists (Popular Socialists) in the same period. Indeed, Castro's rather ludicrous adventurism appalled old-line Communists, who never dreamed that the wild-eyed leader of the abortive attack on the Moncado barracks in 1953 would someday succeed in bringing down the dictatorship of Fulgencio Batista. Thus, in 1957, one of the Cuban Communist leaders, Juan Marinello, publicly repudiated the Castroite policy of "assault on barracks and expeditions from abroad." [2] And, in fact, while scorning Castro, the Cuban Communists—with Moscow's blessings—actually sought for some time to cooperate with Batista, a policy which did not, of course, endear them or their Soviet mentors to the firebrand *Fidelistas*.

In the fall of 1957, however, a new line was worked out at a conference in Moscow of all the world's Communist parties. The statement issued by that conference proclaimed recognition of a new and more favorable situation for the revolutionary movement in Asia, Africa, and Latin America. And under this rubric such parties as the Cuban were advised to stop vegetating and start agitating.[3] In Cuba, this meant that a more positive attitude had to be taken toward the nascent Castro insurgency in the hills of the Sierra Maestra.

The new Cuban Communist approach to Castro took the form of an offer to build a "coalition" of forces. Carlos Rafael Rodriguez, one of the top Communist leaders, was dispatched to the mountains to find Castro and to establish a working relationship with him. To help persuade Castro, Rodriguez took along a quantity of hard cash. After a brief return to Havana, to check with the party high command and perhaps with Moscow, Rodriguez returned to the mountains in September 1958 as an official representative of the Communist Party (the PSP), a development which suggested that a formal bargain had been struck.[4]

Despite this, some considerable distrust between Castro and the Communists persisted. Fidel was everything a traditional Communist was taught to despise: volatile, romantic, adventuristic, and certainly not disposed to subject himself to party discipline. And to Castro the old-line Communist leaders were little better than opportunistic bureaucrats who did the bidding of Moscow and who for years had collaborated with Batista.[5] The "coalition" thus was only a marriage of convenience based on a common aim—power in Cuba.

When that power was finally achieved in January 1959, the alliance between Fidel's 26 July Movement and the PSP began to crumble. In a fashion typical of postwar East European Communists, the PSP leaders began to reach for the levers of power, particularly the mass movements (such as the Trade Union Confederation) and the key positions in the provinces. And they sent up a cry for "unity" for all revolutionaries. Naturally, with a fairly well-established and experienced cadre system, the PSP hoped to absorb the naive and inexperienced guerrilla fighters. But they reckoned without Fidel.

Both the U.S.S.R. and the Cuban Communists were dismayed when Castro went to the United States in April 1959 and spent several hours with Vice-President Nixon. The Secretary General of the PSP, Blas Roca, already nervous about the future course of the revolution, wrote in May that times were "critical", no doubt reflecting fears that Castro was about to adopt a pro-Yankee position. Such fears were fed by Castro's denunciation in May 1959 of the Communists for starting trouble in Oriente Province, where an anti-Communist revolt had broken out within the 26 July Movement.[6]

The old-line Communists felt compelled to defend themselves. They did so by blaming all the troubles in the revolution on so-called "Plattists," (a term derived from the U.S. Platt Amendment and used to brand the opposition with pro-Yankee sentiments). Their actual targets were the non-Communist right wing leaders of the Castro movement. Moscow supported this line; *Pravda,* for example, claimed that "reactionaries" in Cuba were seeking to isolate the "left wing" (*i.e.*, old-line Communists) of the national revolutionary forces.[7]

The Soviets remained generally aloof from Castro until the end of 1959. Khrushchev's visit to the U.S. in September evoked criticism from the Castroites and put the old-line Cuban Communists in the embarrassing position of having to defend the "Spirit of Camp David." Nevertheless, Castro was moving in a general direction that intrigued Moscow, in part because he had broken with some of his most important non-Communist supporters.[8] Thereafter, Castro's relations with the Communists in Cuba became more cordial, and in early November Castro's mouthpiece, *Revolucion*, suggested that Mikoyan, who was then in Mexico, might be invited to Cuba.

To the Soviets, however, the problem of Cuba involved not only the narrow question of relations with Havana but also the much broader issue of how to deal with a host of emerging regimes turning in one way or another toward the Soviet Union. There was Nasser, the first of the lot, and then Kassem in Iraq, Kwame Nkrumah in Ghana, Sekou Toure in Guinea, Sukarno in Indonesia, and a number of lesser lights elsewhere. Until late 1959, the Soviets were content to rest on a strictly pragmatic approach, devoting their policies in the underdeveloped countries primarily toward the removal of the Western presence, the establishment of their own, and the cultivation of correct and cordial governmental relations. Nevertheless, it was becoming increasingly evident to Khrushchev that the U.S.S.R. had misjudged the nature of the new phenomena in the Third World. By and large, the leaders of the regimes which sought Soviet support were nationalists of bourgeois origin. Communists had played little or no role in the various national revolutions, and in some cases had actually been jailed. If indigenous Communists were to come to power anywhere, it would obviously require a long and laborious process of boring from within. In any case, it was clear that these nationalist regimes were not reliable and were not "socialist" in the Soviet sense of the word, even though, at the same time, they clearly were not capitalist. The problem for Moscow thus soon came to be how to keep Soviet obligations to these states within bounds, without in the process losing the benefits of their neutralism and anti-Westernism.

Castro made the problem of avoiding specific commitments, particularly military-security guarantees, especially difficult for Khrushchev and the Soviets. Mikoyan accepted the Cuban invitation and visited Cuba in early 1960, but he avoided any firm commitments when Castro asked for conventional Soviet armaments lest they disrupt the "Spirit of Camp David" and disturb Soviet-U.S. relations on the eve of the scheduled summit meeting in Paris. When that meeting collapsed over the U-2 incident, however, the U.S.S.R. was free to meet (and in fact met) Castro's request and was happy to use Cuba as a new irritant against the U.S.

Soviet-Cuban relations continued to improve, but Castro was not content to let the Soviets set the schedule or determine the agenda by themselves. On the contrary, he was perfectly capable himself of trying to dominate the relationship, without conspicuous deference to Moscow's interests. Thus, in order to bolster his security against the U.S., he deliberately misinterpreted the Soviet position and misquoted Soviet generalizations. In July 1960, for example, Castro was quick to seize on one of Khrushchev's intemperate outbursts against the U.S., rendering a translation of Khrushchev's figurative warning about the protection afforded by Soviet rockets as an ironclad guarantee of the Cuban regime's very existence. Khrushchev, in a calmer moment had to emphasize that this was not the case at all.[9]

As an added embarrassment to Moscow, Castro also seemed to be living proof that the Chinese were right and the Russians wrong. As the Sino-Soviet dispute emerged into the open in 1960, a critical point was whether armed struggle was the preferred road to power. Khrushchev argued no, Mao yes. Thus it was to Khrushchev's advantage to regard Castroism and the Cuban revolution not as a socialist (or communist) upheaval but as the outstanding example of a general trend toward what the Soviet theoreticians came to call "national democracy." [10] This was a new theoretical concept and it suited Soviet policy quite well. Under this definition, regimes such as Castro's were on their way to real socialism but they were not as yet quite "building" it. Thus they did not qualify for full membership in the Communist bloc, with all its attendant rights and obligations, but were considered candidates for membership on their good behavior.

This kind of doctrinal evolution and political caution was understood by some of the old-line Cuban Communists but obviously did not impress Castro. Khrushchev publicly embraced Fidel in New York during the UN session in the fall of 1960, but back home in Moscow the world's Communist parties were approving the concept of "national democracy", citing Cuba as the example, and shunting aside Cuban objections.[11] That this ambiguous theory reflected real Soviet uneasiness about Castro's Cuba was soon confirmed. A few months later Walter Lippman was in Russia on the eve of the Bay of Pigs as Khrushchev's guest; Lippman received the strong impression from Khrushchev that the U.S.S.R. was prepared to write off Cuba and Castro.[12] Khrushchev predicted a Bay of Pigs type of invasion, said it would probably fail, but implied that sooner or later the U.S. would eliminate this hostile intrusion into its sphere of influence.

It was characteristic of the entire relationship between

Khrushchev and Castro, however, that just before the Bay of Pigs Castro resoundingly proclaimed Cuba a "socialist" country.[13] This was surely in part an appeal for some form of Soviet military guarantee, but the Soviets chose at the time to ignore it. Later, of course, Khrushchev was forced to take a second look. Castro had survived the Bay of Pigs, was committing his regime to the Communist bloc in ideological terms, and was working increasingly closely with the Communists at home on practical matters. The questions for Khrushchev were: Could Cuba survive U.S. hostility, and could Castro be relied on as a disciplined Communist? Only time, and Washington, could answer the first. But the Soviets could take some immediate and practical steps concerning the second. They could try to surround Castro with trusted Communists, who could be counted on to restrain his impulses and calm his ideological fervor, hoping eventually to capture practical control of the Cuban political machinery.

By late 1961 the Cuban Communists appeared to be falling in line with Castro. Party leader Blas Roca, at the Eighth Congress of the Popular Socialist Party in 1960, had defined Cuba as merely a "popular progressive revolution," but in the fall of 1961 he sanctioned Castro's proclamation of "socialism" and justified it by asserting that "the people had been asking for a long time for a categorical statement concerning the aims and character of the revolution." [14] Roca's latter statement was published in *Problems of Peace and Socialism,* a journal published in Prague but run by Moscow, and its appearance there suggested that the Soviets no longer objected. Nevertheless, for themselves, the Soviets still took refuge in various euphemisms, such as Cuba's "entering the path" toward socialism. Their hesitation to endorse Cuban socialism unequivocally probably reflected apprehension on a key point: Who would control the new party (the PURS) after it had been organized, the Communists, a known and more or less disciplined group, or the Castroites, who represented a new phenomenon and who were, at best, scarcely disciplined, at least not by Moscow?

It later became apparent that at this juncture the Soviets were waiting to see how the efforts of their man in Havana, Anibal Escalante, would fare. Escalante was number two or three in the old Communist hierarchy, and, more important, in 1961–1962 was in charge of party cadres. When Escalante was purged in March 1962, Castro's indictment of him made it clear that Escalante had been seeking to capture the rank and file of the new revolutionary party, in this way (at least figuratively) to imprison the Castroite leadership.[15] There apparently were leaders in the Communist Party, such as Blas Roca and Rafael Rodriguez, who opposed Escalante (and who survived as a result). It is highly doubtful that a party secretary (Escalante), charged with the sensitive task of organizing cadres, could or would have operated independently and in opposition to Roca unless he had had Soviet support. It was almost certainly no accident, in any case, that the Soviet ambassador to Havana was quickly withdrawn and replaced soon after Castro had ousted Escalante.

Once it became clear that Castro had smashed Escalante's plotting, Moscow must have concluded that a Soviet-sponsored takeover in Cuba (which would probably have left Castro as a figurehead) was no longer feasible, and that, in fact, the old-line Communists were in danger of losing considerable ground if the U.S.S.R. continued to seek control over Castro. Moscow quickly conceded defeat, repudiated Escalante, and threw its full support behind Castro. Not only did it accept his brand of socialism and Marxism-Leninism, it also moved toward accepting Cuba as a regime to be considered at least halfway in the bloc, as illustrated by the new and improved positioning of Cuba in the 1962 May Day slogans.[16]

Castro, magnanimous in victory, was willing to let the Soviets escape blame for the Escalante affair. The stage was thus set for a relationship close enough to permit the installation of Soviet strategic missiles in Castro's Cuba.

The resolution of Cuban-Soviet difficulties, largely on Fidel's terms, in the spring of 1962 coincided with the end of a period of hesitation in Soviet foreign policy which had begun the previous summer. After August 13, 1961, when the erection of the Wall divided the city of Berlin, Khrushchev had been forced by high East-West tensions to retreat from his promise to conclude a separate German peace treaty with Walter Ulbricht by the end of the year and to transfer to East Germany the controls over allied access to West Berlin. (Albanian revelations in later years indicate that Khrushchev had formally committed himself to such a timetable.) The question confronting Khrushchev was whether to be content with what he had already achieved, or merely to await an opportunity to revive his Berlin offensive.

Khrushchev sought initially to probe the Western position in informal discussions with the U.S. which began in the fall of 1961. The talks focused on Berlin access, and the U.S. introduced some new variations.[17] But by March 1962 Khrushchev was growing impatient with haggling over controls, and it is now clear that at about this time he decided to shift over once again to the offensive. Though both he and Foreign Minister Andrei Gromyko continued to pay some lip service to the hope of further bilateral discussion with the U.S., the hard line began to emerge in various Soviet and East German pronouncements. The shift is illustrated by a comparison of two pronouncements issued only a few weeks apart:

> The talks with U. S. Secretary of State Rusk have revealed *the existence of a desire to search for a rapprochement of the position of* [*both*] *sides* with due consideration for the true existing conditions in Germany, although it is quite clear that many obstacles still remain to be overcome. (Gromyko, in an address on April 24, 1962, to a session of the Supreme Soviet.) (Emphasis supplied.)

> It would appear that the statesmen responsible for the policy of the major Western powers . . . have no full appreciation [of the "dangers" in the West Berlin situation.] How else is one to explain the fact that the slightest indications of a sober approach to the solution of the problem of a German peace treaty (etc.) fade away as soon as they appear? . . . Facts show clearly enough that . . . an *unwillingness to soberly assess the situation in Europe appears once more.* (Emphasis supplied.) ("Observer," *Pravda,* May 3, 1962.)

To be sure, the Soviets did not slam the door to further talks, and they continued to toy with various proposals to guarantee Western access, install UN contingents, or set up arbitration arrangements. But it became increasingly clear as the spring progressed that the Soviet position was indeed hardening. One sure sign was a new round of harassments of the Berlin airlanes. In February-March, the Soviets raised a number of new procedural rules in an effort to introduce the East Germans into the air traffic control system, and they backed this with actual physical interference in the air corridors. Though Khrushchev eventually backed away from a confrontation with the Allies, his willingness to probe this most sensitive Western position reflected his larger decision to move toward another Berlin showdown if diplomacy and physical harassment failed to shake the West.

It was in this mood and atmosphere of potential crisis over Berlin that Khrushchev had to consider the situation between Castro and the U.S. In one of his many versions of the missile crisis, Castro has stated that in early 1962 he informed Moscow of Cuban fears of another U.S. invasion.[18] Castro had been alarmed by a vague phrase used by President Kennedy in an interview provided Khrushchev's son-in-law, Adzhubei, which seemed to imply another Bay of Pigs.[19] Castro appealed for help, and he claims that the Soviets in March agreed with his assessment of the U.S. threat. Presumably, Khrushchev was then confronted with specific requests from Castro for a new injection of military hardware, and appropriate negotiations apparently took place between March and the end of June.

According to Castro, the Soviets in these discussions first presented their plan to deploy strategic missiles in Cuba.[20] Precisely when agreement was reached on this plan is not known, although (again according to Fidel) Raul Castro went to Moscow in early July "to discuss the arrangements for installing the missiles." The implication of this is, of course, that some form of agreement had been reached before Raul's arrival. Certainly by mid-July, at the latest, Khrushchev had decided to proceed with this boldest of all his maneuvers to put the West under pressure. Khrushchev's own explanation in late 1962 of the origins of the missile deployment more or less conforms to such a schedule: "The Government of Cuba last summer asked the Soviet Government to provide additional assistance. An agreement was reached about the number of new measures, including the stationing in Cuba of a few dozen Soviet ballistic rockets of medium range." [21]

There are other indications that Cuba, the East-West military balance, and the burden of high Soviet military programs were very much on Khrushchev's mind during this period. It almost seemed as if he were trying to convince himself to go ahead with the Cuban missile scheme. Thus, in May, while on a trip to Bulgaria, he issued threats against U.S. missile bases in Turkey, and he dwelt on a statement by President Kennedy that the U.S. might under certain circumstances strike first with nuclear weapons.[22] In Rumania, in June, he went to great lengths to justify the rise in meat prices in the U.S.S.R., claiming that the alternative was to take funds away from the production of missiles.[23] During the same month, in Moscow, he displayed some concern over possible American reaction to further military assistance to Cuba. He warned his audience—Cubans studying in the U.S.S.R.—that "assistance in arms helps only when these arms are under . . . firm control. . . ."[24]

There was surely some hesitation and debate in the U.S.S.R., about the Cuban missile venture, and the central issue probably was the likely reaction of the United States. The proponents of the move counted heavily on being able to conceal the move and then confronting the U.S. with a *fait accompli*. Once the missiles were in place and operational, U.S. options would be narrowed—destroy the missiles, bargain for their removal, or acquiesce in their presence.

Khrushchev's entire concept of the cold war would probably have led him to minimize the chances of strong, warlike U.S. reactions to the deployment. Certain ground rules of the cold war had gradually evolved over time and had apparently been accepted by both sides. The first rule, reflected in Hungary in 1956, was a mutual respect for the integrity of the opposing bloc's real estate. Once a given area had passed into the opposing sphere of influence and control, the other side could not risk military interference in an effort to regain it. The U.S. had tacitly recognized such a

principle at the time of the building of the Berlin Wall when
—despite the crude illegality of the Soviet move and the existence of U.S. rights in East Berlin—Washington had decided not to move. And the U.S.S.R. had abided by this
proposition during the Bay of Pigs, when Cuba was still
more or less within the U.S. sphere. But now, in 1962, Cuba
had become at least an associate member of the Soviet bloc,
and the U.S.S.R. was now presumably free to make use of
this territory for military purposes, just as the U.S. was in
Turkey. Even if the U.S. were disposed in this instance to
violate the rule, West Berlin was still Khrushchev's hostage.
To Khrushchev, then, a U.S. attack in response to the emplacement of Soviet missiles in Cuba must have seemed unlikely.

There has been much speculation that Khrushchev never
intended to keep his missiles in Cuba, but, rather, always
foresaw a bargain for their removal.[25] This could have been a
fallback position, but Khrushchev had compelling political
and military reasons to prefer the establishment of a permanent missile base to the marginal gain of, for example, trading the withdrawal of his Cuban missiles for U.S. removal
of its Jupiter missiles from Turkey. Moreover, Castro's own
explanation of the purpose of the deployment strongly suggests that the Soviets had sold him the idea on the basis of a
worldwide strategic breakthrough:

> They explained to us that in accepting them [the mis-
> siles] we would be reinforcing the socialist camp the
> world over, and because we had received important aid
> from the socialist camp we estimated that we would not
> decline. This is why we accepted them. It was not in or-
> der to assure our own defense, but first of all to reinforce
> socialism on the international scale. Such is the truth
> even if other explanations are furnished elsewhere.[26]

It has been asserted that Khrushchev was led to believe that the Cuban venture would be a safe risk mainly because of the character of the Kennedy Administration and the nature of its actions and policies prior to the autumn of 1962. For example, it is alleged that Khrushchev took the measure of the President in Vienna in June 1961 and determined at the time that Kennedy's youth and inexperience were major vulnerabilities.[27] Moreover, the Bay of Pigs, the Berlin Wall, and Laos are sometimes cited as examples that the West was "too liberal to fight." [28]

There may be some truth to such analysis, but probably not much. The evidence provided in the Penkovsky papers, for example, suggests an entirely different picture: Khrushchev was frustrated and confused, unable to cope with American reactions, and, in particular, upset by the evident U.S. determination regarding Berlin.[29] If Khrushchev had actually believed that the West could be taken so easily, then the logic of the situation called for a German peace treaty. After all, the physical transfer of control points over Allied access to West Berlin need not have been the dangerous act often portrayed. The U.S. had been prepared, since the days of John Foster Dulles, to accept the physical presence of East German controllers, while ready to deny that this constituted recognition of the East German state. The conclusion seems inescapable that in 1961, and again in 1962, Khrushchev was quite worried by the possibility of a violent American reaction to his challenge over Berlin.

Indeed, the record of 1961–1962 would have suggested to the objective observer not American irresolution but American determination. There was, for example, the tense confrontation of American and Soviet tanks at Checkpoint Charlie in Berlin. And it was Khrushchev who—despite strong Soviet military preponderance on the scene—withdrew his armor first. There was the deployment of American marines in Thailand when the Laotian situation seemed to Washington to take an ominous turn. There was the firm U.S. stand during the dangerous harassment of the Berlin air corridors in early 1962. And, above all, there was the growing realization in the Kremlin that the U.S. and the world at large, understood that there was no missile gap, that, indeed, the true facts of the balance of power pointed in the opposite direction.

The human factor, so difficult to assess in times of international crises, also played an important role in the Soviet decision. Khrushchev prided himself to a high degree on his abilities in personal encounters, and this accounts in part for his penchant for summitry. His massive, thick-skinned ego, his bullying conduct at Vienna, and his general reliance on theatrics suggest sublime confidence that, when face to face with his adversary, he could outpoint him. Thus, he may have convinced himself that when the Cuban crisis broke he would be able to meet the President and talk his way out of trouble. His first, apparently instinctive, reaction in the actual crisis was, in fact, to call for a summit conference.

In sum, because of the urgency of his wants and the intensity of his desire, Khrushchev seems to have persuaded himself that the Cuban gamble was a safe one. The advantages loomed so large to Khrushchev that they overshadowed the legitimate doubts, and this, of course, is one reason why the crisis was so unexpected on the American side. The decisive gains Khrushchev would make were so patently obvious to Washington, and so clearly intolerable, that a vigorous U.S. reaction was simply taken for granted as the other side of the equation. The venture thus had to be ruled out as simply too risky an undertaking for the Soviets even seriously to contemplate. That Khrushchev had been blinded by the glitter of an opportunity to solve all his problems in one bold stroke did not occur to Washington; neither

Soviet need nor Khrushchevian greed were that apparent before the event.

Obviously, Khrushchev was involved in a classic case of miscalculation. But the scribes who have documented the American policy debate during the crisis suggest that the miscalculation was understandable to a degree—*i.e.*, the error was not *complete*, for, in fact, there were some U.S. officials who would have been willing to talk and bargain with Khrushchev. Nevertheless, what Khrushchev underrated in essence was the President's determination not to yield on the principal issue, thus wiping out the crucial ground rule assumed in the Kremlin. Khrushchev also greatly underestimated the tactical advantage which the U.S. held in terms of geography and the local preponderance of power in the Caribbean. When the crunch came, Kennedy, not Khrushchev, held most of the options. Kennedy could apply increasingly greater degrees of pressure, while Khrushchev had only radical alternatives: to capitulate or to raise the ante.

While Khrushchev was in his own mind resolving the problems the missile deployment might someday present, the political scene in Moscow was by no means allowed to lie dormant simply because high-level energies were being concentrated on Cuba. To be sure, Khrushchev had been seized with the idea that Cuba offered him a unique opportunity to display the strength and daring of the Soviet Union, at the direct expense of the power and prestige of the United States, and he clearly expected in this way to advance a variety of Soviet interests abroad. But, at the same time, he also counted on the success of this one bold venture to enable him to score impressively on the home front as well. Indeed, he was apparently convinced that it would almost immediately cure or curb many of his most pressing internal problems and, eventually, help to solve them all. It was this, then, that impelled him to move on the domestic front even as the first of the Soviet strategic missiles were reaching Cuban shores.

What Khrushchev was seeking at home during this period was nothing less than a vast improvement in the performance of the economy, a thoroughgoing modernization of the party system of rule, and, as a prerequisite to both, a great strengthening of his own ability to exercise control over substantive policies and political processes. And for all this he evidently foresaw both the need and the prospect of a breakthrough, a more radical program of change than he had attempted in the past: a basic alteration in the structure and mode of party government, a profound cultural break with the Stalinist past, and a sweeping realignment, or purge, of high-level officialdom. These, at any rate, were the tasks he had in mind in September, when he proposed a fundamental realignment of the party apparatus, and in October, when he encouraged the beginning of an unprecedentedly strong campaign against Stalin.

Khrushchev in early September proposed in a private note to the CPSU Presidium that all provincial and local party organs be split into two hierarchies, one to oversee industrial production and the other to supervise agricultural activities.[30] This highly unorthodox scheme was no doubt actually intended by him to improve the administration of the economy, but it also seems to have been designed to "reorganize" some of his bureaucratic and political opposition right out of existence. Together with a number of other measures (including the formation of a new Party-State Control Commission), the division of the party was intended to give Khrushchev and his most faithful followers on the CPSU Secretariat greater direct control over party cadres and, through them, the economy itself. Indeed, as

Richard Lowenthal has commented, Khrushchev undoubtedly was seeking through this reorganization to deliver a
blow against both "the oligarchic cohesion of the party bureaucracy in general and against the authority of the Presidium in particular." [31]

Later in September, *Pravda* suddenly announced the
"discovery" of some 44-year-old writings by Lenin which
were extraordinarily appropriate to Khrushchev's plans in at
least two respects.[32] First, Lenin is said to have asserted that
economics, not politics, were of prime importance in the Soviet Union. From this it was easy to infer, as Khrushchev
subsequently did, that the party, hitherto organized on a ter-
ritorial (*i.e.*, largely political) basis, should be restructured
on the basis of a "production" (*i.e.*, economic) principle.[33]
Second, Lenin allegedly had had something to say about the
political effects of this economic primacy: "In accordance
with the need for economic leaders, a certain re-evaluation
of leaders should be carried out, a certain reshuffling of them
so long as it is not possible for them to adapt themselves to
new conditions and new tasks." [34] From this it was easy to
infer the obvious and to apply it to Khrushchev's time as
well as Lenin's.

That Khrushchev was indeed contemplating "a certain
reshuffling" of leaders was confirmed in October by the re-
appearance, after a year of relative disuse, of the most awe-
some political weapon at his command, de-Stalinization. On
October 21 (the day before the missile deployment to Cuba
was revealed by President Kennedy), *Pravda* published the
vigorous and highly emotional anti-Stalinist poem, "Stalin's
Heirs," by one of Khrushchev's improbable favorites, Evgeny Yevtushenko. The poem, alluding to Stalin's reluctance
to remain within his coffin, charged that some Soviet leaders
still in office publicly professed anti-Stalinist sentiments but
privately pined for a Stalinist revival.[35]

Shortly thereafter, the famous account of life in Stalin's slave labor camps, *One Day in the Life of Ivan Denisovich*, was published, to the intense excitement, pro and con, of the entire literary community.[36] It was quickly rumored at the time, and has since been confirmed, that the publication of these two works had been approved by Khrushchev personally.[37] And it was widely believed, as reported by Priscilla Johnson, that "a new round of de-Stalinization . . . was about to begin" and that "the jobs, and perhaps even the lives, of those who had assisted the [Stalinist] terror were now in peril." [38]

Thus, by late October, the atmosphere in Moscow was characterized by ferment and anticipation of great change. That this atmosphere had been deliberately cultivated, and that there was a purpose in such cultivation, can hardly be doubted. Indeed, it now seems likely that Khrushchev had planned to unwrap his complete program later in the year at a plenum of the Central Committee. Perhaps he had even seriously considered doing this in the afterglow of a trip to New York, where, as has been suggested, he could have triumphantly announced to the UN, and to the U.S., the establishment of his strategic missile base in the Caribbean. But as it turned out, Khrushchev had no victories to proclaim and no reason to travel to New York to celebrate them. Probably as a direct result, when the plenum convened in November, he had no new policy of de-Stalinization to declare and no new shakeup in the leadership to announce.

NOTES

1. Dwight D. Eisenhower, *Waging Peace* (New York, 1965), pp. 520–525.

2. Theodore Draper, *Castro's Revolution* (New York, 1962), p. 54.

3. U.S. Senate Committee on the Judiciary, "The Communist Threat to the U.S. Through the Caribbean," Part III, November 1959, Testimony of General C.P. Cabell, pp. 162–64.

4. Draper, pp. 54–56.

5. Boris Goldenberg, "The Cuban Revolution: An Analysis," *Problems of Communism*, September-October 1963, p. 7.

6. Draper, p. 63; Andres Suarez, "Castro Between Moscow and Peking," *Problems of Communism*, September-October 1963, p. 18.

7. *Pravda*, May 12, 1959; Current Digest of the Soviet Press, Vol. XI, No. 19, p. 34.

8. Draper, pp. 26, 65–69.

9. Suarez, p. 20.

10. The term "national democracy" was incorporated in the Statement of Communist Parties issued in December 1960; the Soviet interpretation appears in an article by Boris Ponomarev, "Concerning the National Democratic State," *Kommunist*, No. 6, May 1961. See also Ye. Bochakarov, "New Paths for New States," *New Times*, No. 41, October 1961.

11. Cuban objections to national democracy are mentioned by Herman Matern in *Neues Deutschland*, December 23, 1960.

12. Walter Lippman, *The Coming Tests with Russia* (Boston, 1961).

13. Suarez, p. 22.

14. For Blas Roca's position in 1960 see *Problems of Peace and Socialism*, November 1960. For his defense of Castro see *Problems of Peace and Socialism*, October 1961.

15. Draper, *Castro's Revolution*, pp. 201–205 ff.

16. *Pravda*, April 9, 1962.

17. Richard P. Stebbins, *The United States in World Affairs* (New York, 1963), pp. 79–86.

18. Castro's interview with Jean Daniel in *The Washington Post*, December 11, 1963.

19. Kennedy-Adzhubei interview, *The New York Times*, November 29, 1961.

20. Daniel, *Washington Post*.

21. *Pravda*, December 13, 1962.

22. *Pravda*, May 17, 1962.

23. *Pravda*, June 20, 1962.

24. CDSP Vol. XIV., No. 22, pp. 6–7.

25. For a critical discussion of such speculation, with references, see Arnold Horelick, *The Cuban Missile Crisis*, The RAND Corp. Memorandum RM 3779-PR, September 1963, pp. 8–12.

26. *Ibid.*, p. 22.

27. Elie Abel, *The Missile Crisis* (Philadelphia, 1966), p. 36.

28. Arthur Schlesinger claims that this phrase, usually attributed to Khrushchev, was in fact a distortion by Robert Frost of Khrushchev's remarks. Arthur Schlesinger, Jr., *A Thousand Days*, p. 821.

29. Penkovsky, p. 216.

30. "Note to the Presidium of the Central Committee CPSU Concerning the Reorganization of the Party Leadership of Industry and Agriculture, September 10, 1962," *Stroitelstvo Kommunizma v SSSR i Razvitiye Selskovo Khözyaistvo* (The Construction of Communism in the U.S.S.R. and the Development of Agriculture), Moscow, Vol. 7, April 1963, pp. 163–177.

31. Richard Lowenthal, "The Revolution Withers Away," *Problems of Communism*, XIV, January-February 1965, p. 12.

32. "New V.I. Lenin Document," *Pravda*, September 28, 1962.

33. Khrushchev introduced this proposal to the Central Committee in November, claiming on the basis of the Lenin dis-

covery that "now there is a question, perhaps for the first time in the recent history of civilized peoples, of an administration in which not politics but economics assume predominant significance." (Moscow Domestic Service, November 20, 1962.)

34. *Pravda*, September 28, 1962.

35. Among Yevtushenko's prime targets may have been the conservative Frol Kozlov, de facto "second secretary" of the party; see Priscilla Johnson's excellent study, *Khrushchev and the Arts* (Cambridge, 1965), p. 46.

36. Priscilla Johnson notes that publication of Solzhenitsyn's *One Day* . . . in *Novy Mir* must have been authorized no later than September 21, 1962, the date the journal was signed to the printer. (*Ibid.*, p. 5n.)

37. *Ibid.*, pp. 5, 6.

38. *Ibid.*, p. 5.

3. The Crisis

THE CUBAN MISSILE CRISIS has already been used as a sort of textbook study in American crisis management, and understandably so. The memoirs of inside observers and the work of diligent journalists contain considerable information and insight as to how American policy was formulated and implemented in those critical October days. But, predictably, there have been no comparable recapitulations from the Soviet or Cuban side. Khrushchev's rationale for Soviet conduct was embarrassed and apologetic, and Castro's was angry and defiant. And Khrushchev's successors, to whom one might turn for revelations, have so far been of no help. Yet it is clear that this momentous crisis was a turning point both for Khrushchev and his policies; neither he nor his program were ever able to recover fully from his defeat at the hands of the U.S.

In a sense, the Cuban missile crisis began in Berlin. It was here, at any rate, that Khrushchev made his first important mistake, by allowing the Berlin situation to get out of hand—and to affect his Cuban plans—before he was ready for any kind of confrontation with the U.S.

During June and July, 1962, the Soviets gradually began building up diplomatic pressure for a German peace treaty. Khrushchev summoned a meeting of the Warsaw Pact, and on June 7 that body issued a declaration approving further discussions with the U.S., but at the same time intimating that the Communist states would soon conclude a separate treaty with Ulbricht.[1] Simultaneously, the Soviets protested against "provocations" around the Berlin Wall. The three Western Allies responded by proposing a four-power discussion on ways to regulate tensions in Berlin.[2] Obviously, Khrushchev could not agree to such narrow talks because they would imply a continuing four-power responsibility for both East and West Berlin, and this would demolish his entire campaign to eliminate the "remnants" of the four-power occupation.

The matter might have rested there for the time being had it not been for a grisly incident. On August 17, 1962, a young East German named Peter Fechter attempted to escape over the Wall and was shot down by East German guards. Mortally wounded, he lay dying for some hours before the eyes of helpless onlookers. The West Berlin public was outraged and turned its wrath on the most immediate symbol of Communist authority, the hapless Soviet soldiers who daily entered West Berlin to guard the grotesque Soviet war memorial near the Brandenburg Gate. Soviet buses carrying these guards to and from duty were stoned, and some tense moments followed.

The Allies again insisted on immediate four-power talks.[3] To head off this increasingly attractive approach to a now dangerous situation, the Soviets countered on August 22 by abolishing the job of their military commandant for Berlin, one of the last vestiges of the old four-power occupation of the city, and transferring his responsibilities to the commander of the Soviet forces in Germany.[4] An East German commander for East Berlin was then appointed, and this carried with it the threat that Soviet policy would henceforth be to force the Western powers to accept East German control over allied movement between the two parts of the city. The Soviets then resorted to the use of armored cars to carry their soldiers to the war memorial in West Berlin; this was a provocative and offensive reminder to Berliners of the disparity between the Soviet rejection of Allied rights in East Berlin and the continuing Soviet exercise of corresponding rights in West Berlin.

By early September, the high state of tension in Berlin threatened Khrushchev's broader scheme for combining the Cuban and Berlin issues at the proper moment, that is, after the Cuban missile deployment had been completed. Che Guevara was in Moscow discussing the Cuban situation and, most probably, going over the strategy of the missile deployment. Khrushchev was concerned at this moment to avoid any clash in Berlin which might conceivably draw U.S. retaliation in Cuba. Though he had carefully avoided linking the two issues in any way, he had to recognize that the effect of the tensions in Berlin was to reinforce U.S. concern over the arms buildup in Cuba.

Khrushchev thus took steps to pull the Berlin situation back under his tactical control. On September 4, Ambassador Anatoly Dobrynin informed the President, through Attorney General Robert Kennedy, that out of deference to the President, and in view of U.S. congressional elections in November, the U.S.S.R. would cause no trouble in Berlin or in Southeast Asia.[5]

Though the U.S. was at this point still ignorant of Khrushchev's intentions and officially discounted the chance of an "offensive weapons" deployment to Cuba, the extensive buildup of Soviet arms in Cuba was becoming increasingly evident. It was also becoming more embarrassing to the Administration. Growing suspicions about the nature of the buildup led to more U.S. high-altitude reconnaissance, and on August 29 Soviet surface-to-air (SAM) missile sites were discovered on the island.[6] This news called for a Presidential statement, since the President had only recently cast doubt on any emplacement of SAMs in Cuba. The statement was issued on September 4 and not only revealed that the U.S. had good knowledge of the character of the Soviet arms buildup thus far, but also included a warning that must have greatly upset Khrushchev's calculations:

> There is no evidence of any organized combat force in Cuba from any Soviet bloc country; of military bases provided to Russia; of a violation of the 1934 treaty relating to Guantanamo; of the presence of offensive ground-to-ground missiles; of other significant offensive capability either in Cuban hands or under Soviet direction and guidance. *Were it to be otherwise, the gravest of issues would arise.*[7] (Emphasis supplied.)

Here, then, was direct evidence that the U.S. would not look the other way while Khrushchev prepared an "offensive" capability in Cuba. Indeed, the U.S. drew a sharp line between "defensive and offensive." The Soviets were aware, of course, that this warning had come too late, *i.e.*, after the whole machinery of the missile deployment had been set in motion. Strategic missiles were already on the way, and some had almost reached Cuban shores; thus, despite their probably intense concern at this point—no doubt heightened by press speculation that the U.S. might throw a blockade around Cuba—the Soviets had little choice but to proceed.

Khrushchev's apprehensions must have been further aroused by the intrusion of a U.S. patrol plane into Soviet territory in early September.[8] Though the U.S. immediately

admitted an accidental violation and reaffirmed the Eisenhower commitment to refrain from reconnaissance flights
over the U.S.S.R., the incident could easily have been mis-
read. Khrushchev might even have suspected that the U.S.
was preparing another humiliation similar to the U-2 incident of 1960.

Khrushchev's suspicion and concern may have been further sharpened by the general content of President Kennedy's warning against offensive deployments to Cuba. The
warning was based on the limited evidence available in
Washington, but Khrushchev, in possession of all the facts,
may have wondered whether the President was deliberately
downplaying the importance of what had already happened
(*i.e.,* the great buildup of Soviet forces in Cuba), in order to
leave the U.S.S.R. a way out, or, conversely, to entice it into
a trap. Finally, in this chain of events, Khrushchev could not
have failed to be alarmed at the President's announcement
on September 7 calling up the reserves.

But whatever Khrushchev's misgivings at the time, he
clearly decided to brazen through. He began, in fact, to re-
sort to a desperate stratagem, which, in the end, only compounded the American reaction. He began to lie.[9] A Soviet
statement of September 11 took refuge in the ambiguity of
"offensive" versus "defensive" weapons. And, at a time when
Soviet medium-range missiles (MRBMs) had actually been
in Cuba for some days, Moscow claimed the entire military
reinforcement of Castro was "designed exclusively for defensive purposes." [10] Further:

> The Government of the Soviet Union also authorized
> TASS to state that there is no need for the Soviet Union
> to shift its weapons for the repulsion of aggression, for a
> retaliatory blow, to any other country, for instance Cuba.
> Our nuclear weapons are so powerful in their explosive

force and the Soviet Union has so powerful rockets to carry these nuclear warheads, that there is no need to search for sites for them beyond the boundaries of the Soviet Union.[11]

This statement of September 11 was an extraordinary document for it virtually catalogued all the worries bedeviling Khrushchev: the threat of a blockade; the overflight incident; the call-up of U.S. reserves; the tensions over Berlin; and the contradiction between U.S. reaction to the military buildup in Cuba, on the one hand, and Soviet acquiescence in U.S. bases around the Soviet Union, on the other. In retrospect, the statement even strikes a plaintive note, suggesting a man caught in a dangerous dilemma and protesting the injustice of it all:

> They [the Americans] have brought armaments there in their ships, and these armaments, stationed along the frontiers of the Soviet Union . . . are said to be there lawfully, by right. They consider this their right. But to others the U.S. does not permit this even for defense. . . . What conceit! Equal rights and equal opportunities must be recognized for all . . . ! [12]

On September 13, the President sought to discount rumors of (and a public outcry for) an invasion, which may have relieved Khrushchev somewhat, but at the same time the President repeated his warning against the deployment of Soviet strategic weapons. There the matter rested for a time, at least in public. There were exchanges between Gromyko and Adlai Stevenson at the UN, and a stream of speculation in the U.S. press, but the Soviets for the most part remained quiet. Indeed, words alone had little meaning at this point; the buildup in Cuba was reaching the critical point.

In the face of this new statement by President Kennedy, Khrushchev could have played the deployment of the missiles in two ways. He could have slowed down the rate of deliveries and waited until the surface-to-air missile system was completed and brought into operation, in this way masking the deployment of strategic missiles from the prying eyes of the U-2. Or he could have ordered the entire operation into high gear, refusing to wait for maximum secrecy and, instead, gambling everything on speed. He chose the latter course, which was certainly in keeping with his character, presumably because his original calculations were already becoming unstuck. The U.S. was reacting far in advance of the Soviet schedule. *Inter alia*, there was the threat of a blockade, which would cut across the lines of supply and trap the missile buildup halfway. And there was even a threat of direct attack, particularly since the U.S. had begun some preliminary military deployments in the southern part of the U.S.

But if events had already thus conspired to upset Khrushchev's timetable, his decision to gamble on speed was responsible for the greatest blow of all. It was responsible, in fact, for U.S. detection, on October 14, of the Soviet threat still in an early stage of the buildup. The intermediate range missiles (IRBMs) which could cover most of the U.S. had not yet been delivered, but the medium-range missiles (MRBMs) were being rushed into operation even before the SAM system had become fully operational (and this despite the obvious increase in U.S. overflights).[13] As it turned out, the Soviets were caught with about six MRBM sites (of four to six missiles each) ready for operation and three IRBM sites (and a probable fourth) just begun and not scheduled for completion until December 15.[14] One can only wonder at the possible outcome of the subsequent crisis if the U.S. had discovered the deployment only after, say, some 6o-odd missiles were ready to fire.

Just before the discovery of the ballistic missiles, and before the U.S. had begun the agonizing process of planning a riposte, Khrushchev left Moscow for a barnstorming tour of the provinces. The greatest triumph or humiliation of his career was in the works, but he coolly left town to check on the harvest, and the harvesters, and to maneuver for support of his plan to split the party into two separate industrial and agricultural entities.[15]

During these critical days, when the first missile sites were actually being constructed, many of the top Soviet leaders were out of sight. Mikoyan did not appear in public; Brezhnev, Yury Andropov, and Khrushchev's son-in-law, Adzhubei, were in Yugoslavia; Boris Ponomarev, a party secretary, was in Italy; and Petr Demichev was in East Germany. Kozlov, Alexei Kosygin, Dimitry Polyansky, and Mikhail Suslov were on the job in Moscow, receiving the usual stream of visitors. News from Cuba was played in a low key, and no one could have guessed from the pages of *Pravda* that a great international crisis might be brewing.

But once Khrushchev had returned to the capital, the tempo picked up. On October 11, *Pravda* published the full text of a speech made at the UN by President Osvaldo Dorticos of Cuba, who warned of U.S. plans for attacking Cuba. The next day *Pravda* published a speech by Castro and news reports of U.S. planes attacking Cuban ships and buzzing the Soviet tanker *Druzhba*. A Presidium meeting on the 12th is suggested by the presence in Moscow on that date of all the Presidium members, both full and candidate, excluding only Mikoyan, but including even those normally in their republican capitals.[16]

On the following day, Ambassador Dobrynin in Washington took pains to reassure Robert Kennedy and Chester

Bowles that Khrushchev would not cause trouble during the congressional elections.[17] On the same day, *Pravda* ostentatiously announced that Khrushchev had received the Chinese ambassador, who was soon to leave his post, and had held a "friendly" conversation with him. This was the first of several gestures to the Chinese during the crisis; Khrushchev subsequently gave a dinner for the ambassador, and *Pravda* published a long article on China prominently displaying a message of greeting from Mao Tse-tung to Khrushchev.[18] Suslov later claimed that Khrushchev had at this time offered to wipe the slate clean and to renew friendly relations with Peking.[19] Khrushchev, aware of his coming problems with the U.S., had chosen to create an impression of a possible rapprochement with Mao. He was unaware, however, that the Chinese were about to drive across the Indian frontier.

While Khrushchev and his wife were entertaining the Chinese ambassador at dinner on the evening of October 14, two American U-2 reconnaissance planes were recording the telltale evidence that an MRBM site was under construction at San Cristobal in Cuba. The missile crisis had begun; that evening top officials in Washington were quietly being told of the momentous discovery. The same evening the first snow of the winter fell on Moscow. Khrushchev spent the following day entertaining the President of Finland, Urho Kekkonen, and that evening Khrushchev and his wife attended a ballet performance. If Khrushchev had any inkling of what was happening in Washington, he certainly gave no sign of it.

As the Kennedy administration began to debate and to divide, Khrushchev continued to entertain President Kekkonen. The two men had breakfast together at the Finnish Embassy on October 16, attended the opera in the evening, and on the next day met at a final dinner held in Kekkonen's honor. Kozlov and Kosygin were also in evidence during this period, but, surprisingly (unless he was ill), Brezhnev did not appear in public during the Kekkonen tour.

During this same period, Khrushchev somehow found the time to extend further reassurances to Kennedy. He called in Ambassador Foy Kohler on October 16 and explained that the announcement by Castro on September 25 that the U.S.S.R. would construct a "fishing port" in Cuba was a blunder.[20] Had he, Khrushchev, been in town at the time, he would not have allowed the announcement to be made because he wanted to avoid causing trouble for the President during the elections.

But the more immediate problem for Washington was how to deal with Gromyko, who had come down from New York to see the President on October 18. It was decided not to confront Gromyko with the evidence, but to allow him ample opportunity to reveal the truth. The President even read from his public statements of September 4 and 13 about Soviet offensive weapons in Cuba, but Gromyko did not blanch. Rather, he hinted that Khrushchev might want to meet with the President later in the year.[21]

There is no evidence of exactly when the Soviets realized what had happened in Washington, though the chances seem quite good that Khrushchev was pretty much aware by October 19 that he had been caught. The Soviet military in Cuba must have observed the marked increase in U-2 flights.[22] (On October 15, *Pravda* had carried reports out of Havana about U.S. overflights.) The Soviets must also have detected at about this time the beginning of some military movements in the southern U.S. Finally, the report Gromyko sent to Moscow, on October 18 or 19, must have noted the special attention the President had paid to Cuba in their conversations and the pointed references to the question of offensive weapons there. Since Moscow knew exactly how far the missile construction had progressed when Gromyko met the President, it is likely that the top Soviet officials would have suspected that Washington had begun to smell a rat.

The crisis finally broke into the open on Monday evening, October 22, when President Kennedy informed the world of Khrushchev's bold move into Cuba. The immediate Soviet reaction to the President's statement was not particularly enlightening. The Soviets were clearly stalling for time, apparently in the hope that specific American intentions would be clarified. Poor Valerian Zorin at the UN obviously had no instructions from Moscow other than to dissimulate, which he did manfully but with great embarrassment.[23] The Soviets must have known the United States had photographs to prove its case but probably believed that the U.S. would not show them. Thus they still could hope to cast doubt on the American accusations and perhaps sway enough opinion in the UN to wring some concession out of Washington, or at least delay the implementation of U.S. countermeasures.

The Soviet leaders finally churned out the expected fare: a government statement, orders to Marshal Rodion Malinovsky to be on guard, and a report of "consultations" with the Warsaw Pact allies to put themselves in a state of readiness.[24] At the same time, the Presidium made quite a show of solidarity, turning out en masse for a dinner honoring the visiting Rumanian first secretary, Gheorghe Gheorghiu-Dej, and for the opera, *Boris Godunov*. Oddly enough, Khrushchev at the same time made a small gesture to the U.S. by going out of his way personally to congratulate an American performer in the opera, Jerome Hines. All of this was featured on the front page of *Pravda* on October 24.

But, despite some bluster, there was a faint air of shakiness in the Soviet position that first day. At the UN, the Soviet draft resolution proposed Soviet-American negotiations on Cuba for the "purpose of restoring the situation to normal and thus removing the threat of an outbreak." [25] The phrase "restoring to normal," in retrospect at least, seemed to contain the germ of a deal Khrushchev was turning over in his mind.

But Khrushchev could not turn anything over for very long. A major decision was pending: If the Americans instituted their naval "quarantine"—as threatened by the President—what orders would be sent to the Soviet arms carriers steaming toward the picket line? The U.S. formal proclamation was issued on the morning of October 24 when Soviet ships were only a few hours away.

It is characteristic of Khrushchev's style that at this critical moment he reached out for an audience. The unsuspecting victim was William Knox, president of Westinghouse Electric International who happened to be visiting Moscow. Khrushchev summoned him to the Kremlin that same afternoon for three hours of "threats, complaints, and peasant jokes." [26] Khrushchev appeared in a state of near exhaustion, but he warned that if a Soviet ship were sunk, Soviet submarines would go into action. Perhaps Khrushchev thought Knox would sound the alarm to the American Embassy, which in turn might warn Washington to veer from its perilous course. Perhaps Khrushchev was only relieving his own frustrations and tensions. In any event, despite his sharp words to Knox, Khrushchev refused to accept the challenge of the U.S. blockade. At around midnight, Moscow time, about a dozen of the Soviet ships turned away from the confrontation. Thus, sometime between about 4 P.M. and midnight, the choice had been made.

What preceded this decision, what took place that evening in Moscow, will probably never be known. Certainly, the decision was not an easy one. Yielding in the first significant test with the U.S. certainly weakened the Soviet position. On the other hand, a clash at sea was particularly disadvantageous for the Soviets. Despite Khrushchev's threat of Soviet submarines, the Caribbean was a bastion of American naval power and a confrontation in this area might well have led to a Soviet humiliation.

Though sharp debate within the Soviet leadership at this first crucial turning point cannot be demonstrated, there are some odd bits of evidence which suggest that political maneuvering within the Kremlin was intensifying. First, there was a sudden change in the Soviet position on the India-China border war, and then there was an odd piece of political byplay involving Khrushchev himself. On October 25, *Pravda* (a morning paper which usually is set for the printers by midnight, Moscow time) published a firm endorsement of the Chinese side in the border fighting which had broken out with India. This was a dramatic shift from official Soviet neutrality (and unofficial sympathy for India). *Pravda* and *Izvestia* published the full text of a Chinese government statement, and *Pravda* offered this startling endorsement:

> As for the Soviet people, they see the statement of the Chinese government as evidence of sincere concern over relations with India and eagerness to bring the conflict to a halt. The proposals made by the Chinese government are in our opinion constructive.

Izvestia offered similar fare:

> The Soviet people view the new statement of the CPR as an important manifestation of good will . . . it is necessary to emphasize the constructive spirit of the CPR (Chinese Peoples Republic) proposals to conduct nego-

tiations on the border issue without prior conditions. It would be true statesmanlike wisdom if the Indian side showed a proper understanding of the peace-loving initiative of the CPR.

Much later, after the Cuban crisis was long past, Khrushchev violently denounced the Chinese attack on India. It is worth considering, therefore, that this endorsement on October 25 represented a setback for Khrushchev. It could be that supporting China was only a tactical gambit to worry the U.S. and the world at large, but it is also possible that Khrushchev was deferring to the Presidium rather than improvising policy as he went along. In any event, the simultaneous decision not to run the blockade and to abandon Soviet neutrality in the Indo-China skirmish, albeit temporarily, suggests some horse trading and jockeying within the Kremlin.

Another strange event on the same date, October 25, also seemed to cast something of a shadow over Khrushchev's position. The Ukrainian Supreme Soviet on that date passed a decree renaming a small city in Kirovograd Oblast: the city of Khrushchev was redesignated Kremges. That someone in Kiev, the Ukrainian capital, would wish to raise such a sensitive subject—with all its anti-Khrushchev implications—is suggestive of political maneuvering. Certainly no one would be likely to take such an action without first checking with someone in Moscow, and Moscow's approval at this highly delicate moment in the Cuban crisis suggests a deliberate slap at Nikita Sergeyevich. Though an announcement of the change was not published at the time, an official decree of this sort would have been widely known, and was, in any case, subsequently (in mid-November) published in the Moscow organ of the U.S.S.R. Supreme Soviet.[27]

Whatever restraints may have been imposed on Khrushchev by the collective leadership, they were not as yet clearly evident in Moscow's handling of the crisis itself. Soviet ships turned away from the U.S.-imposed quarantine line, but work on the missile sites themselves continued, and no break appeared in the official Soviet position. The duel between Zorin and Stevenson continued in the UN. Khrushchev advanced various schemes, but all of his proposals left the Soviet missile deployment untouched.

On Friday, October 26, the first important break occurred in the Soviet position. This was the mysterious private letter from Khrushchev to the President proposing, in effect, the withdrawal of the Soviet missiles, in return for a lifting of the quarantine and a U.S. guarantee not to invade Cuba. This first letter was followed within a day by a second letter which added a new condition, withdrawal of U.S. Jupiter missiles from Turkey. Considerable speculation about the situation in Moscow was prompted by this change of position in the second letter. Did Khrushchev deliberately raise his price, in response to hints in the American press that such a deal was possible? Did the collective leadership impose restraints on Khrushchev after learning of his bold initiative to end the crisis? Was there confusion and disarray in Moscow?

The most likely explanation of Soviet conduct is that the first letter was almost completely a personal initiative by Khrushchev which received little or no coordination in the Presidium. When its contents became known, cooler heads prevailed and the price was raised. Khrushchev had to agree to such a deal, in light of internal political pressures and continuing Western speculation that the U.S. would have to make some concessions. The Soviet Embassy in Washington and the Soviet Mission at the UN would have reported corridor chatter and press speculation that the Jupiter missiles in Turkey were expendable, and this surely suggested to some Soviets that the U.S. could be persuaded to go along with an essentially face-saving maneuver. But whatever support the Turkish-Cuban bargain may have had in the Kremlin, it quickly evaporated when the U.S.S.R. was subjected to new pressures and warnings from the U.S., a process which suggested that at least no *massive* opposition had developed to Khrushchev's leadership. At a minimum, however, it probably can be said that Khrushchev's highhanded, personal diplomacy, particularly his use of private channels, caused concern among his colleagues, and was one more black mark against him for future reference.

The case for a personal initiative in the first private letter rests in great part on the description of the letter as very much Khrushchev's own. Unfortunately, the full text has never been published, but the unmistakable Khrushchevian stamp apparently is firmly imprinted on all its pages.[28] Khrushchev's personal initiative, outside of regular channels, also seems evident in the famous secret encounter between A.S. Fomin of the Soviet Embassy—thought to be the chief of Soviet intelligence in Washington—and the American reporter John Scali of the American Broadcasting Company.[29] This meeting resulted in a private Soviet overture for a compromise settlement, along the lines eventually agreed upon. It coincided closely in timing and substance with the first Khrushchev letter, and it seems likely that the two moves were intended by Khrushchev to be read in conjunction with one another, as indeed they were.

While the U.S. was pondering the strange letter and Scali's report, Moscow presumably received a cable from Fomin indicating Washington's interest in Khrushchev's package deal. At the earliest, Fomin's report was received about 3 A.M. in Moscow and was thus available for the morning business discussion. This is significant because, de-

spite Fomin's report of U.S. interest, the decision was nevertheless taken to send a new letter to Washington, canceling
out Khrushchev's private letter and proposing the Cuban-
Turkish missile base deal.[30] There was an obvious urgency
about the second letter. It was immediately broadcast from
Moscow, whereas Khrushchev's first letter was still unknown
to the public.

Trading American missiles for Soviet missiles, which was
the key element in the new letter, had been alluded to all
during the crisis. The most intriguing reference to such a
potential bargain appeared in the armed forces' newspaper
Red Star, on October 27.

> The U.S.A. demands the removal from Cuba of Soviet
> military equipment provided to her exclusively for de-
> fense purposes. *Why then not remove American military
> equipment and troops from the hundreds of military
> bases ringing the Soviet Union?* Cuba is very close to
> the territory of the U.S.A., it is hypocritically pointed out
> in Washington. They took care to note this. "But what
> about the American bases near the frontiers of the Soviet
> Union?" asks the Swedish newspaper, *Stockholms Tid-
> ningen.* "Could the Russians, citing the American prece-
> dent, not resort to action to eliminate the threat that, as
> they say, is aimed against them?" [31] (Emphasis added.)

Whether this represented Soviet military pressure on the
politicians to stand their ground cannot be said with assur-
ance. But it does appear that the military was expounding
the precise line which was then reflected in the second letter
to Washington. Two days earlier, on October 25, *Red Star*
had printed statements by Marshal Malinovsky which some
observers interpreted as a sharp criticism of the political organs, perhaps reflecting the old rule that "when the Soviet
Army faces action, it turns against its controllers." [32]

In any event, the Turkish missile deal was more than a passing fancy. It received heavy Soviet publicity. Not only was Khrushchev's second letter immediately broadcast but the full text was also published in the Soviet press, plus maps indicating the extent of American bases around the Soviet Union. Fomin's reaction, when confronted by Scali with the apparent reversal and betrayal, was agitated and confused. His reaction suggests that the second letter was not a well-thought-out gambit, but a last-minute effort to obtain better terms. Since Fomin was apparently a KGB agent, the fact that he was not fully informed about the second letter also suggests a return to regular formal channels of communication. Thus, the second letter was a deliberate reversal of Khrushchev's initiative and reflected the "collective" leadership in action.

Washington's handling of these two confusing documents is well known. The decision was made to ignore the second and deal with the first. The answer was sent out that evening and received in Moscow sometime early Sunday morning. Of decisive importance, however, was the personal role of Robert Kennedy, who handed Ambassador Dobrynin a copy of the letter and a warning that time was running out and that the U.S. was prepared to take "strong and overwhelming retaliatory action" by the first of the week.[33] Dobrynin was pessimistic that Moscow could agree to American terms, but this warning was promptly conveyed to Moscow.

It can only be imagined what agonizing debates took place on Sunday in Moscow. By early afternoon the crisis reached its climax. Khrushchev accepted U.S. terms. He had little choice. Dobrynin's warning, probably received early Sunday morning, indicated time was short; American military deployments must have been obvious to even the most casual diplomatic observer in Washington. Reports from all over the world must have been flying back to Moscow indicating the U.S. was not going to back down. Indeed, Khrushchev, in later trying to explain away the crisis, laid heavy emphasis on the extreme urgency of the moment:

> On the morning of October 27 we received information from our Cuban comrades and from other sources which directly stated that this attack would be carried out within the next two or three days. We regarded the telegrams received as a signal of utmost alarm, and this alarm was justified. Immediate actions were required in order to prevent an attack against Cuba and to preserve peace. A message was sent to the U. S. President which suggested mutually acceptable solutions.[34]

This explanation is interesting in that it is an indirect criticism of the Turkish-Cuban deal. If in fact, Moscow did receive signals of alarm on the morning of October 27, the raising of the price in the second letter was done after these signals had been received. Perhaps, with the crisis well past when he delivered this rationale, Khrushchev felt it necessary to remind the authors of the Turkish proposal how close they may have come to disaster.

In any event, by Sunday evening world tensions had subsided greatly. President Kennedy dryly quipped that perhaps he should go to the theater. For his part, Khrushchev did go to the theater. A great array of Soviet leaders turned out with him: Brezhnev, Kosygin, Kozlov, Mikoyan, Polyansky, Suslov, Demichev, Leonid Ilyichev, and Alexander Shelepin. Perhaps this was intended to be a demonstration of unity at the top in the aftermath of crisis and retreat. But perhaps, deliberately or not, it was also symbolic of the emergence of a new and more effective collective surrounding the defeated Khrushchev.

NOTES

1. *Izvestia,* June 11, 1962.
2. Stebbins, *The United States in World Affairs,* pp. 83–84.
3. *Ibid.*
4. *Pravda,* August 23, 1962.
5. Abel, *The Missile Crisis,* p. 19.
6. U.S. Senate, Committee on Armed Services, "The Cuban Military Buildup," 1963, p. 6.
7. David L. Larson (ed.), *The "Cuban Crisis" of 1962* (Boston, 1963), Doc. No. 1.
8. Stebbins, p. 85.
9. For Khrushchev's private but false reassurances to President Kennedy's aides see Theodore C. Sorensen, *Kennedy,* pp. 252–253. Public denials were also bald. *New Times* (No. 37, September 12, 1962), for example, published an article entitled "Hysterical Washington, Calm Havana," which accused the U.S. of coming out "with the wholly false story of Soviet troops landing in Cuba and setting up missile bases there."
10. Larson, Doc. No. 5, p. 7. For the timing of the arrival of Soviet missiles in Cuba, see Abel, pp. 24, 41, and U.S. Senate, p. 7.
11. Larson, Doc. No. 5.
12. *Ibid.*
13. U.S. Senate, p. 7.
14. *Ibid.*
15. Khrushchev's speeches and activities during this tour are contained in *Pravda* daily and in *Khrushchev's Collected Works on Agriculture,* U.S. Department of Commerce JPRS: 20,900, September 1963.
16. *Pravda,* October 13, 1962.
17. Abel, p. 50.
18. *Pravda,* October 14, 1962.

19. M.A. Suslov, "Struggle of the CPSU for the Unity of the World Communist Movement," *Soviet Documents*, Vol. II. No. 16, April 20, 1964.

20. Abel, pp. 49–50. Sorensen, p. 779.

21. The question has often been raised whether Gromyko knew about the missile deployment at this time. Normally, one would expect the foreign minister to be informed of such matters, and indeed later, after the crisis, Gromyko dwelt on the charge of deception and virtually admitted that he had known. It might be noted that this was the man who, as Khrushchev once said in Gromyko's presence, would pull down his trousers and sit on a keg of ice for as long as he was ordered to do so.

22. U.S. Senate, p. 7.

23. Larson, p. 90.

24. *Pravda*, October 24, 1962.

25. Larson, p. 59.

26. Abel, p. 151.

27. *Vedomosti Verkhnovo Soveta*, No. 46, November 16, 1962, p. 1088.

28. The first Khrushchev letter is paraphrased in Abel, p. 177; Sorensen, p. 803.

29. The Scali-Fomin affair is described in Abel, p. 175; *Washington Post*, August 4, 1964.

30. *Pravda*, October 28, 1962.

31. A. Leontyev, "Ashes and a Cold Shower," *Red Star*, October 27, 1962.

32. R. Conquest, *Russia After Khrushchev*, (New York, 1965), p. 180.

33. Sorensen, p. 806. Abel, p. 199.

34. *Pravda*, December 13, 1962.

4. The Aftermath of Retreat

THE DEFEAT IN CUBA came as a great shock to the Soviet leadership. Perhaps the greatest single blunder in Soviet peacetime history, it is small wonder that many within the elite came to ask themselves how it could have happened. And surely, in seeking an answer to this painful question, they had first to subject the principal architect of the Cuban venture to a new and much more critical kind of scrutiny. They may have secretly concluded that—as publicly charged by the Chinese—Khrushchev had been guilty of "adventurism" when he deployed the missiles and "appeasement" when he withdrew them. In any case, the Soviet failure in Cuba came to be Khrushchev's failure. The point was, and in fact would remain, that, whatever his reasons, Khrushchev had grievously erred and could only be expected to pay the appropriate penalty for the fact.

Indeed, beginning in December 1962, and continuing through at least mid-April 1963, Khrushchev seems to have faced an increasingly dubious and perhaps hostile Presidium. The policies and declarations of the time seemed to reflect a pronounced drift to the non-Khrushchevian "right," *i.e.*, in the Soviet political spectrum, toward the positions of the party "conservatives." Many of Khrushchev's plans and proposals were stalemated or reversed. The campaign against the liberal intellectuals reached a shrill frenzy and involved even a partial posthumous rehabilitation of Stalin himself. Khrushchev's various administrative reorganizations were criticized, postponed, or subjected to major amendment, and his program to channel more and more funds into an expansion and modernization of the chemical industry seems to have been largely forgotten, to the temporary benefit of more traditional areas of investment, such as the steel and defense industries. And, finally, a leader of the party, Frol Kozlov, who served as a spokesman for conservative interests, seems to have made a bid of his own for the party First Secretaryship.

The first post-Cuban signs of discontent within the Soviet leadership appeared in the immediate wake of the crisis, within days of Khrushchev's promise to President Kennedy on October 28 to remove the Soviet missiles. To many in the party the first order of business surely was the politically ominous and wide-ranging question of de-Stalinization, and it was in this area that the initial move seems to have been made. On November 1, *Pravda* reprinted an article from the Mongolian party newspaper which, in the Soviet context, could be read as a warning to Khrushchev to call off his anti-Stalinist campaign and to abandon his hopes for a shakeup in the leadership.[1] Two days later, in an apparent followup, *Pravda* published an article signed by the aging Marshal Klimenti Voroshilov (himself a Khrushchev victim) which suggested more of the same and which seemed to propose the possibility of a bargain of sorts, *viz.*, support for Khrushchev's Cuban policy in exchange for suspension of de-Stalinization.[2]

Khrushchev apparently deemed it prudent not to reject

this sort of bargain, and, perhaps in order to insure the survival of other elements of his program, he later seemed reluctantly willing to give up (or, more likely, postpone) his de-Stalinization campaign. Though the liberal writers and artists continued to press their cause, the campaign rapidly began to fizzle out. By late November, the Central Committee received, apparently sympathetically, a petition from a group of conservative and neo-Stalinist artists who complained about the appearance of "revisionist" works in the public media, asked for party intervention to prevent growing "formalist" trends, and even, according to one source, "set out to demonstrate that the party's 'soft' cultural line had contributed to the degenerating international situation." [3] The presentation of this petition marked the "first link in a long chain" that, within months, "was to see Party conservatives destroy the recent liberal trend in art, then literature, in an attempt to halt the process of de-Stalinization and perhaps even upset the balance of power inside the Communist Party." [4]

Khrushchev managed to survive the November plenum of the Central Committee without immediately visible scars in other areas of policy. He pushed through the reluctant Committee his plans for party reorganization. (The whole scheme was, of course, thrown out the window in one of the first official acts of Khrushchev's successors in the fall of 1964.) [5] It was not long after this, however, that signs of trouble began to multiply. Khrushchev, it seemed, would have a larger price to pay for his failures in Cuba and elsewhere than the mere abandonment of his plans for de-Stalinization and self-aggrandizement. It became increasingly clear that concern and dismay, initially aroused by his revival of impassioned anti-Stalinism and by his handling of the missile crisis, had been compounded by his radical plans for administrative restructuring and by his evident willingness to subordinate the party's needs and prerogatives to the requirements of the economy.[6] And, of greatest ultimate import, it was apparent that the ambitions of his opponents and potential opponents had been stimulated by all the above and by his concomitant loss of prestige and self-confidence.

More stimulated than most, and in a better position to do something about it, was Khrushchev's heir apparent and the party's de facto "second secretary," Frol Romanovich Kozlov. Kozlov's high position in the hierarchy, his long experience as a professional party manager, and his reputation as a practical, yet ideologically orthodox, executive, all served him in good stead. So too, apparently, did his personal qualities. President Eisenhower, who met Kozlov in New York and Washington in 1959, for example, found him to be a "personable, yet obviously tough and capable man." [7] Others found him to be "amiable, but impervious";[8] shrewd and ruthless, with a tough but "limited" mind;[9] an efficient man who "bellowed" in jovial moments, but who had the sound of "a man chewing firecrackers" when speaking to underlings.[10]

Vice-President Nixon also met Kozlov in 1959. The following exchange between the two men—in which Kozlov pointed to disagreements within the Soviet leadership—took place at a Blair House reception for Kozlov in July, 1959:

> *Nixon* (addressing Mr. Kozlov): When it comes to foreign policy, Mr. [Christian] Herter [the Secretary of State] and I speak as one. You understand that, don't you?
>
> *Kozlov:* Truth is born out of argument. . . . There is never a day we [in the Kremlin] don't argue.
>
> *Nixon:* The difference is we publicize our arguments.

Kozlov: You would publicize differences between you and Mr. Herter?

[Mr. Nixon grinned and the conversation took another turn.][11]

The Vice-President had been given this opportunity to fence with Mr. Kozlov, and the President had had his chance to size him up, only because Nikita Khrushchev—before making a trip to the United States—had wanted two of his top lieutenants to reconnoiter in depth. (Mikoyan had come to the U.S. before Kozlov.) Kozlov had, in general, made a good impression during his visit. His toughness, noted above, apparently did not upset his hosts (with the possible exception of Vice-President Nixon), while his political skills favorably impressed them, perhaps in part because, contrary to expectations, he could be at least superficially charming: "He is probably the only citizen in the entire Soviet Union who wears a button-down shirt. . . . If he worked in New York, he'd probably live in a fancy suburb and drive a sports car. He has the Leningrad manner. . . . [*i.e.*] the airs of a sophisticate—and a veneer of Western European culture." [12]

Kozlov's charm, like his collar, however, was deceptive. He was, essentially, a hard-working Soviet bureaucrat who was, in the words of Leon Volkov, "ruthlessly pursuing the star of power. . . . [and] too busy traveling the high road to explore the byways." [13] Indeed, his whole background had served to limit his horizons but encourage his ambitions. One of nine children (of whom five died in childhood and two during the war), Kozlov, born in 1908, was the son of poor Russian farmers. He became a party member at age 18, then attended and graduated as a metallurgical engineer from the Leningrad Polytechnic Institute in 1936. Too young and inconspicuous to be caught in Stalin's sweeping purges of the mid-1930s, Kozlov on the eve of the German invasion became a party secretary in Leningrad's famous "Izhevsk" steel and armaments plant. Before the war's end, he was transferred to the party Central Committee in Moscow.

After the war, in 1948–49, partly through luck and partly through skill, he benefited from the outcome of a vicious rivalry between two party titans, Andrei Zhdanov and Georgi Malenkov. Zhdanov died suddenly in 1948 and Malenkov moved ruthlessly to purge Zhdanov's followers in Leningrad. Kozlov not only escaped this purge but for a time became one of Malenkov's proteges, and in 1950 he was appointed first secretary of the city of Leningrad. Demoted in the immediate aftermath of Stalin's death, he soon made a comeback, this time under the personal aegis of Khrushchev, who sponsored him for the post of first secretary for the entire Leningrad region.[14] His career continued to prosper as Khrushchev maneuvered against Malenkov, and in June 1957, after having sided with Khrushchev against the anti-party group, he became a full member of the Presidium.

Cold, clever, and ambitious, perfectly capable of siding with Malenkov against Zhdanov, then Khrushchev against Malenkov, Kozlov was nonetheless a parochial man. He was, in his ideas, in his ideology, completely cautious and wholly conventional. He was also the party man entire, dismayed, perhaps even outraged, by the impulse and imagination of Khrushchev, at least insofar as these qualities were brought to bear on the structure, elan, and function of the professional party bureaucracy.

But Kozlov's narrow party regularism and his Leningrad background did not redound completely to his advantage. The former did not necessarily appeal to those of a somewhat less conservative persuasion, probably including Brezhnev. Nor was it likely to attract leaders who—while loyal party members—had risen to prominence principally through their services within nonparty bureaucracies. Such leaders included Kosygin, who had spent most of his career in one or another of the government economic organs.

Moreover, Kozlov's Leningrad heritage could only lead to skepticism on the part of Moscovites, such as Shelepin, and suspicion among Ukrainians, such as Nikolai Podgorny. Indeed, it is well within the realm of possibility that these potential drawbacks were among the *advantages* seen by Khrushchev in his selection of Kozlov as his heir apparent, *i.e.*, were qualities which in Khrushchev's mind reduced the chances of Kozlov's becoming a premature heir in contention. But if so, Khrushchev had reckoned without the shock of the retreat in Cuba and had underestimated the ability of his "second secretary" to move quickly and effectively to take advantage of that shock. In fact, Kozlov, who as a senior Soviet official had as much to mourn in the wake of Cuba as anyone else, paused hardly at all in memory of fallen policy. And, perhaps partly as a consequence, he came within the narrowest margin of getting rid of his chief a full eighteen months before his confreres on the Presidium actually did so.

The first issue exploited by Kozlov in the aftermath of Cuba probably was Khrushchev's scheme to divide the party into independent agricultural and industrial entities. Controversy over this question seems to have been particularly intense almost from the very moment of its approval by the Central Committee in November. It was not long, in any case, before resistance to the new measure compelled the publication of a number of revealing articles which defended the reorganization, Khrushchev's economic and doctrinal rationale for it, and even, indirectly, Khrushchev's personal leadership of the party. *Pravda* in late December admitted that "certain Communists" feared that the decisions of the November plenum had "contradicted the established principles of party construction." [15] *Izvestia,* in early February, protested that the split in the party organs could "in no way weaken the party leadership of this [worker-peasant] alliance." [16] And *Partinaya Zhizn* (*Party Life*) revealed during the same month that "several comrades say that [improving economic performance] is not a matter of organizational reconstruction, but of the intelligent use of economic levers." [17]

The most complete and interesting defense of the program appeared in late January in *Ekonomicheskaya Gazeta.*[18] An article in this paper sought to handle criticisms of the program which were not otherwise publicly discussed until November 1964—*i.e.,* after the post-Khrushchev leadership, in its first major policy move, had disowned the reorganization and announced its impending dissolution.[19] The article sought to answer two questions which, it confessed, had been raised as a consequence of Khrushchev's proposal: "Whether we do not reorganize the leadership of the economy rather too often?" and "Whether this thesis [Lenin's alleged concept of economic primacy] does not contradict another well-known Lenin utterance concerning the correlation of policy and the economy in the conditions of the Soviet state?" It also sought to confound the critics of Khrushchev's personal style of leadership by citing Leninist precedents for two of Khrushchev's most objectionable practices, personal intervention in detailed economic and administrative work and vindictive assaults on those who stood in his way. "Lenin [too] directly led the country's economic life by daily resolving a mass of various urgent economic questions. He [too] personally directed the work of organs of economic administration. . . ." And he too, "in struggling resolutely against the slightest violations of state discipline, called for the 'persecution' of bureaucrats and everyone who obstructed economic life. . . ."

While the Soviet press thus rose occasionally to the defense of Khrushchev's program, its tone and substance during much of January and February seemed on the whole to lack direction. Certainly, after a round of Republican and provincial party meetings in December, there were few signs of the enthusiastic kind of propaganda campaign one might have anticipated in the wake of an important Central Committee decision. The new doctrine of "economics over politics" was no longer discussed, and the new emphasis on the priority of the chemical industry was allowed to subside. The statutes for the Party-State Control Commission were published, but relatively little was made of them, and in some respects they seemed to give the new agency fewer powers than Khrushchev had originally intended.[20] Other announcements of decrees implementing the decisions of the November plenum were duly made, but these often seemed perfunctory or confused or were, in several instances, subsequently rescinded.[21]

Similarly, concerning the cultural scene, there was no easily discernible party line during much of December and January. Until late in the latter month, when a neo-Stalinist revival began clearly to dominate, it was a "time of paradox, of patent indecision at the top." [22] Altogether, on the domestic scene, it was as if Khrushchev had retained enough energy, guile, and power to forestall a full-scale political assault—partly, it seems, by himself "joining" the opposition—but not enough to press forward with his own program or to prevent effective attacks on particular aspects of his policies.

By late February, when elections to the Supreme Soviet necessitated a round of "campaign speeches," Khrushchev's general discouragement with the trend of events had become quite apparent. His speech to his constituents on February 27 was both emotional and pessimistic.[23] It alluded darkly to the need to spend "enormous" sums on "military might," offered the Soviet people little in the way of praise for past performances, and promised virtually nothing in the way of future improvement. And all this, of course, came from a man who had once insisted—and would again in the future insist—that the U.S.S.R. had already satisfied its defense requirements and who had once been lavish in his praise of "socialist" accomplishments and in his pledges of glories to come.

In contrast, Kozlov, speaking in Leningrad the day before Khrushchev, had hailed the U.S.S.R.'s great success and remarkable prospects and described Soviet society as the "brightest and most joyous on earth." [24] Moreover, Kozlov seemed to give only grudging and qualified approval to Khrushchev's plans for the chemical industry and called for large new investments in the machine-building industry, a demand contrary to the spirit of Khrushchev's remarks to the November plenum and a demand which was to be specifically disallowed by Khrushchev in April.

On March 8, Khrushchev addressed a meeting of writers.[25] Apparently under specific pressure from conservatives, including Kozlov, Khrushchev had only harsh words for the assembled intellectuals, demanding that they follow narrow party-formulated rules for literature. Insisting on conformity must have pained him deeply, not, of course, because he respected free creative endeavor, but because, in the process, he was forced to recant in a most sensitive area of politics and policy. In effect, he had to repudiate his own cultural policy of some years' standing, *viz.*, minimal party interference in the arts and tacit permission for the appearance of literary works more realist than socialist. More important, he had to revise his own previous assessments of Stalin, pay tribute to Stalin's merits and services, contradict his earlier statements implicating the anti-party group in Stalin's crimes, and, in general, reverse the anti-Stalin campaign inaugurated by him only a few months before.

The next blow to Khrushchev's prestige and power came on March 13, when an unusual joint meeting of the party Presidium and the Council of Ministers decided—without any prior warning whatsoever—to establish a Supreme National Economic Council charged with solving all "questions connected with the work of industry and construction and . . . the fulfillment of state plans" and empowered to give "orders and instructions" to all appropriate state bodies, regardless of their subordination.[26] This move—of a magnitude which normally would have involved a decision of the Central Committee as a whole[27]—was out of the ordinary in several respects. Neither the press nor the leadership subsequently devoted much space or time to an examination of its functions or, as would seem to have been in order, praise of its virtues. Khrushchev himself avoided comment until late April, and then his remarks were not only unenthusiastic but included some pointed criticism of the council's chief, D. F. Ustinov, for his performance in his previous job of running the nation's defense industries.[28]

Moreover, by virtue of its centralized powers and the appointment of a strictly state-oriented official as its head, the establishment of the new Supreme Council appeared to shift emphasis away from greater party management of the economy.[29] It also concentrated in this new organ specific administrative powers assigned by the November plenum to the existing top state economic organs, and, in contradiction to Khrushchev's injunction at the same plenum, gave to these organs direct authority over comparable bodies in the union republics.[30]

It was disclosed in late March that this drift away from Khrushchevian administrative concepts and economic policies was, in effect, scheduled to continue indefinitely. *Pravda* of March 31 informed its readers that high-level planning officials had recently convened (at the behest of the same

Presidium–Council of Ministers meeting which had established the new Supreme National Economic Council) to discuss economic plans for 1964, 1965, and 1966–1970. The decisions of these officials—which presumably reflected guidelines laid down in speeches to the group by First Deputy Premiers Kosygin and Ustinov—failed to give any meaningful priority to the chemical industry, and, at the same time, re-emphasized the regime's interest in such traditional areas of investment as electric power and the machine building industry.

Khrushchev left Moscow in late March for a delayed vacation on the Black Sea. While he was still away, *Pravda* announced on April 9 that the next plenum of the Central Committee would be concerned with ideology. Such an agenda was unprecedented in the post-Stalin era, and the decision apparently had been made by the Presidium in Khrushchev's absence. It may have been engineered by Kozlov and inspired by the Presidium member most concerned with ideology, Suslov. In any case, the announcement obviously flew in the face of Khrushchev's explicit demand in November 1962 that the next plenum deal with the development of the chemical industry.[31]

It was also while Khrushchev was absent from Moscow that the central party apparatus, presumably including the Presidium itself, seems to have deliberately repudiated his wishes in yet another area, concerning a matter of great doctrinal import, the status of maverick-socialist Yugoslavia. His belief that Yugoslavia was building socialism was a matter clearly of some considerable importance to Khrushchev; he had asserted it more than once from the public rostrum. Speaking as recently as December 1962, for example, he had asked the Supreme Soviet, "How can we ignore the fact that the peoples of such a country [Yugoslavia] are building socialism?"[32] But astonishingly, on April 8, *Pravda*, publishing the annual slogans for May Day, revealed that precisely this "fact" had been ignored; the slogan for Yugoslavia omitted the obligatory reference.

"Fraternal greetings to the working people of Yugoslavia," the relevant slogan read in full. "May the friendship and cooperation of the Soviet and Yugoslav peoples grow stronger in the interests of the struggle for peace and socialism." Obviously missing was any mention whatsoever of the all-important *building* of socialism. This omission in the carefully considered last word of the Central Committee indicated quite clearly that, Khrushchev's earlier statements notwithstanding, the U.S.S.R., in common with the Chinese Communists and the Albanians, continued to refuse to recognize the legitimacy of Yugoslav socialism.[33] It should have been perfectly clear to all concerned that this slogan, as worded, represented a significant defeat for the First Secretary.

The week before the publication of the slogans, eight full members of the party Presidium had assembled in Moscow without Khrushchev, ostensibly to greet a delegation of visiting French Communists.[34] At no other time since the death of Stalin had so many of the principal leaders publicly gathered in the absence of the party chief. Further, the presence of this many members hinted of a business session of the Presidium which, *inter alia*, might have been expected to review the forthcoming slogans for May Day. Kozlov, in Khrushchev's absence and as de facto "second secretary," would presumably have been in the chair.

Kozlov may have chosen this particular occasion to make an overt move against Khrushchev. If so, he had picked a good time and a promising issue. Khrushchev's position was already at low ebb, and the question of Yugoslavia had various broad and embarrassing implications for the First Secretary personally. Not only did the Khrushchev-inspired rapprochement with Belgrade represent a central issue in Sino-Soviet contention, it also touched on Moscow's relations with its client states in Eastern Europe and even the direction (right or left) of the U.S.S.R.'s domestic policies. Moreover, as Kozlov was surely aware, Khrushchev's attitude toward Tito and the Yugoslav experiment was distinctly unpopular among the more orthodox members of the Soviet party; Kozlov himself, and the party's two leading ideologues, Suslov and Ponomarev, had in the past been notably unenthusiastic about endorsing Yugoslav socialism.[35]

If Khrushchev had been outvoted or deliberately ignored by his colleagues on the Presidium, concerning both the agenda of the next Central Committee meeting and the question of the May Day slogan on Yugoslavia, his reaction when he received the news in Gagra could not have been entirely amiable! Indeed, it may have included a sudden—and perhaps literally heart-rending—confrontation with Kozlov. Though not announced until the following month, on April 10, Kozlov apparently suffered the heart attack which eventually was to kill him. Immediately thereafter, in a move without precedent, the Yugoslav slogan was officially revised and reissued; it now specifically credited Yugoslavia with "building socialism." This was on April 11, and it is a matter of public record that Kozlov's last public appearance was made the day before.[36]

The conservative consolidation of Soviet policies during the first three months or so of 1963 was by no means confined to the domestic scene. There seems to have been a parallel retrenchment of foreign policies along essentially non-Khrushchevian lines. In broad terms, this assumed to some degree a Kozlovian "isolationism" which stressed traditional Soviet and Marxist verities concerning the aggressive designs of the "imperialist enemy" and which placed renewed emphasis on the priority development of the bases of Soviet national power, the heavy and defense industries. Accordingly, while, in keeping with a more conservative outlook, there were no provocative or incautious moves against the West during this period, the tone of Soviet propaganda grew more militant and the attitude of the Soviet government toward the West became more hostile. The U.S.S.R. indicated in this way, and through diplomatic activities as well, that it was neither anxious to improve relations nor optimistic about even long-range opportunities to do so.

Earlier, however, during December and a part of January, Khrushchev had indicated that in the wake of the Cuban crisis he would prefer a period of East-West accommodation and that he was prepared to take some steps to move the prospect closer. This apparent desire was no doubt prompted in part by his appreciation that there were few areas in which Soviet foreign policy was likely to make appreciable gains, at least so long as international relations remained tense and the memory of Soviet perfidy and Soviet capitulation in the face of superior power remained vivid.

In any event, Khrushchev's speeches and interviews during December and part of January reiterated the case for international understanding. In mid-December, though in some ways bellicose, he delivered a plea for peace and spoke of the "mutual concessions" made "soberly" by the U.S. and the Soviet Union during the Cuban crisis to prevent a third world war.[37] In an interview he granted on December 31, he remarked that he agreed with declarations to the effect that "it was necessary to embark courageously and resolutely on a constructive review of unsettled international problems and to untie the knots of dangerous tensions which could cause new crises."[38] In mid-January, he asserted that "most clear-headed representatives of the Western countries . . .

are forced to admit more and more often that disputes with the socialist countries must be settled by negotiations and not by war." [39]

Khrushchev's first important post-Cuban foreign policy move was a conciliatory one. Reversing the usual Soviet position, he proposed in a private letter to President Kennedy on December 19 that a test ban agreement be concluded on the basis of two or three on-site inspections.[40] It is probable that he genuinely sought at this time to find some means—perhaps the test ban—to ease East-West tensions. The situation vis-à-vis the Chinese had been growing worse since the previous spring and had become alarmingly bad after the Cuban episode; Khrushchev in December seemed to be preparing the way for a formal break with Peking, and under these circumstances would surely have wished troubles with the West to ease.[41] At the same time, pressures on the domestic economy were growing more acute, and relief would demand the diversion of some investments and skilled manpower away from heavy industry and the military.

A test ban would have had the virtue, then as well as later, of offering Khrushchev a clear-cut issue to use against Peking, and perhaps would also have helped to facilitate a transfer of resources to the civilian economy. In any case, new moves against the West (as, for example, against West Berlin) no doubt appeared to be, after Cuba, unduly risky and not very promising. On the other hand, new appeals to the West for understanding and cooperation—which were, after all, a part of the Khrushchev tradition—may have appeared both timely and potentially fruitful. To Khrushchev, it may have seemed to be a time, not for licking old wounds, but for pretending that nothing had really changed.

But if Khrushchev in December had been seriously interested in easing cold war tensions, there was little evidence in late January that the sentiment had persisted. Secret U.S.–

Soviet test ban talks begun in midmonth collapsed two weeks later, primarily because of Soviet inflexibility.[42] At the same time, the Soviet press began to step up its anti-Western propaganda, and official Soviet statements began to reflect a harder anti-Western position.[43]

This change in line coincided with a sharp turn to the "right" taken in both the ongoing debate between liberal and conservative intellectuals and the attitude of the party toward that debate. On January 20, a liberal writer, Viktor Nekrasov, was prominently attacked in the Moscow press for his articles on the United States and Italy which had been published in late 1962 and for his "dangerous" view of the East-West dispute as, allegedly, a kind of "fifty-fifty" proposition. One paper alleged that Nekrasov had, incomprehensibly, failed to see the "war psychosis fanned by the imperialist circles," and another condemned him for his "attitude of compromise" and his inability to recognize the "unbridled reign of militarism" in the U.S.[44] A week later, *Pravda* printed a vicious parody of a 1962 poem by Evgeny Yevtushenko and, in effect, linked the Soviet liberals with the Western imperialists; the poem contained a formula which suggested, as noted by Priscilla Johnson, that "the West equals abstract art, and a liking for either equals treason." [45]

The most sensational and politically sensitive aspect of this resurgence of conservative views emerged on January 30, when *Izvestia* published an attack on Ilya Ehrenburg, the internationally known, and internationalist-inclined, liberal author. The *Izvestia* piece was notable principally because it highlighted Ehrenburg's admission, made in his memoirs published in 1961 and 1962, that he and others— presumably including Khrushchev—had known at the time of Stalin's crimes but had felt compelled to live with this knowledge in silence. The man responsible for resurrecting this issue, a conservative hack named Vladimir Yermilov, had almost certainly been politically inspired and wished, at a minimum, to embarrass Khrushchev.[46]

While the liberals were subjected to mounting invective, and Khrushchev himself came under veiled attack, a flurry of press statements, official remarks, and diplomatic notes indicated that Khrushchev's post-Cuban talk of "mutual compromises" and negotiations with "sober-minded" Western leaders had been superseded by a quite contrary spirit. Official notes to Bonn and Paris on February 5 warned that the U.S.S.R. would consider the nuclear arming of the West German Bundeswehr as a direct threat to its "vital national interests," an unprecedented use of this phrase.[47] *Pravda*, on February 7, asserted that anti-Cuban hysteria was being fanned in the U.S. And in mid-February the U.S.S.R. officially denounced U.S. underground nuclear testing and warned of possible consequences.[48]

This new militancy was further developed in speeches by Defense Minister Malinovsky and Frol Kozlov which painted unusually grim pictures of the international climate and prospects for negotiated settlements. It was almost as if they were directly refuting the initial post-Cuban approach of their own First Secretary. Thus, Malinovsky, speaking on Soviet Armed Forces Day:

> The U.S.A. and its closest allies, regarding war as a means of settling international disputes, are steadily intensifying the militarization of the economy. . . . They have surrounded the socialist countries with many military bases. . . . The events in the Caribbean finally opened the eyes of those who still continued to believe the lying American propaganda. . . . The threat of nuclear war was averted, but this must not induce complacency in us or blunt our vigilance. . . . It must not be naively supposed that the imperialists have laid down

their arms. Greater vigilance is demanded of us today than ever before.[49]

Kozlov was equally strident. Indeed, a comparison of the election speeches of Brezhnev (still Khrushchev's man) and Kozlov on February 26 reveals considerable differences in emphasis; in general but unmistakable terms, Kozlov emerges as distinctly at odds with, and harder than, Brezhnev (and thus presumably Khrushchev) concerning relations with the West and on the specific issues of Cuba, Berlin, military spending, and the question of the chemical industry vs. the steel industry.[50]

Khrushchev, in his previously mentioned election speech of February 27, was himself more than adequately militant. But, unlike Malinovsky and Kozlov, Khrushchev explicitly related domestic welfare to defense spending and the failure to achieve an "agreement" with the West. In this way, he certainly implied the *desirability* of an accommodation with the West, if not the feasibility.

> If the international situation were better, and if it became possible to reach an agreement and to shed the burden of armaments, this would multiply the possibilities for a further upsurge of the economy and for raising the living standards. . . .
>
> It is necessary to state frankly: when the government reviews the question of . . . where to direct how much of the available resources, difficult puzzles often have to be solved. On the one hand, it would be desirable to build more enterprises that make products for satisfying man's requirements . . . , to invest more in agriculture, and to expand housing construction. On the other hand, life dictates the necessity for spending enormous funds on maintaining our military power at the required level. This reduces and cannot help but reduce the people's possibilities of obtaining direct benefits.

The anti-Western campaign reached something of a high point in early April. It was then that the Soviet Foreign Ministry delivered a note to the Allies which declared that "facts show that in their strategic calculations the governments of the Western powers rely not on a peaceful settlement of the main problems . . . but on achieving some kind of a superiority in the arms race, and ultimately on the use of force." And the note warned that Western plans, if implemented, would rule out even disarmament *talks* for at least the next ten years.[51]

The first glimmering of a change in the Soviet attitude toward the West and of a resurgence of Khrushchev came on April 11, the day the Yugoslav May Day slogan was amended and the day after Kozlov's last public appearance. *Pravda* of that date reprinted an article from the *Washington Post,* and, while this of itself was unremarkable, the appearance through this means of praise for President Kennedy's "sincere efforts" to reach an agreement with the U.S.S.R. was a startling departure from the editorial norm. That this one reference was more than happenstance seemed to be confirmed soon thereafter by the journal *Kommunist,* which in mid-April published yet another long-lost Lenin document, this one pointing out the occasional need of the U.S.S.R. to make concessions to the "bourgeois powers" in the interest of Soviet economic development.[52]

Strong hints of a more conciliatory Soviet attitude were provided throughout May. Khrushchev agreed early in the month to hold talks about a possible test ban treaty with the U.S. and Britain, and, in general, Soviet interest in the matter seemed to be reviving.[53] A note addressed to Bonn and Paris on May 17 again protested the implications of Franco-German rapprochement, but in a much more restrained manner than its predecessor of February 5 and without ref-

erence to "vital national interests." [54] In late May, Walter Ulbricht of East Germany revised the prevailing line that a
solution of the German question would ease the way for
other settlements, including disarmament, by declaring instead that a German peace treaty could not be concluded
without a prior agreement on "at least a test ban." [55] And all
this was, of course, subsequently dramatized in mid-June by
the sudden ending of Soviet jamming of Western radio
broadcasting, and capstoned in July with the open failure of
Sino-Soviet talks and the conclusion of a limited test ban
treaty with the U.S. and Britain.

Signs of a return to Khrushchevian policies abroad were
paralleled by symptoms of a similar revival in domestic policies and a general refurbishing of the First Secretary's political image. On April 17 *Pravda* seemingly prepared for Khrushchev's impending return from vacation with a panegyric
reviewing a collection of his speeches entitled "A Major
Contribution to the Theory and Practice of Communist Construction." The editorial claimed that the publication of
Khrushchev's works constituted a "significant event in the
life of our party and the country," and gratuitously hailed
Khrushchev's 22nd Party Congress as, together with Lenin's
2nd and 8th Congresses, "the most outstanding event in the
history of the Communist Party of the Soviet Union and of
the whole world communist and workers movement."
Throughout the article, emphasis was placed on the wisdom
and success of such traditional Khrushchev policies as priority for agriculture, the need for material incentives, and the
"welfare of man." [56] This apparent revival of concern for the
consumer was echoed three days later in a small, front-page
item in one edition of *Izvestia* which announced a decision
of the Supreme National Economic Council to increase by
one billion rubles the planned production of consumer goods
in 1963.[57]

Khrushchev spoke in Moscow on April 24 to a gathering of construction and industrial workers.[58] As he was in his election speech in February, he seemed bitter, but now his mood was demanding rather than defensive. He seemed to be roasting those who had ruled during his absence. He lamented the sorry state of economic management, insisted that something be done about it, and criticized the heads of the top economic organs by name. He reiterated his belief in the virtues of the chemical industry and announced, cryptically, that the Central Committee had decided to convene a plenum at some unspecified date to deal with this subject. Finally, he attacked the line toward the machine building industry advocated by Kozlov in February.[59]

A return to Khrushchevian economics was also suggested by a revival in late April, after three months of almost complete silence, of press interest in Lenin's purported thesis concerning economics over politics.[60] The return was confirmed on June 4 when *Pravda* announced that the Premier had made a number of proposals concerning "basic principles and approaches for drafting the economic plan for 1964–1965 and following years." Khrushchev, *Pravda* said, had declared the need for a "fundamental revision" in planning and had asserted that the chemical industry should be the chief beneficiary of such a revision; consumer goods, agriculture, and industry (in that order) would benefit in turn.

Khrushchev's comeback could also be seen in developments associated with the Central Committee meeting on ideology. Initially scheduled for late May, it was announced in mid-May that the plenum had been postponed some three weeks, and this announcement had been preceded by numerous signs that the party's strident campaign against writers had been considerably toned down.[61] Indeed, with minor exceptions, the truly virulent attacks against the recalcitrant writers had ceased by mid-April, within days of Kozlov's last public appearance.[62] In any event, the plenum actually signaled the end of the campaign and the restoration of a more Khrushchevian approach to the arts and the artists.[63]

NOTES

1. *Pravda*, No. 1, 1962. The Mongolian paper *Unen* had denounced a recently deposed Mongolian leader who had tried to exploit the "struggle against the cult of personality" for his own "far-reaching selfish aims," including a purge of the Mongolian party leadership. The analogy with Khrushchev and his plans in this otherwise gratuitous reprint was obvious. See Carl A. Linden, *Khrushchev and the Soviet Leadership 1957–1964* (Baltimore, 1965), p. 158.

2. The Voroshilov article supported Khrushchev's decisions concerning Cuba but claimed in reference to the "errors and distortions" of Stalinism that "now all this lies behind us" (thus, among other things, giving the lie to Evgeny Yevtushenko's quite specific assertions to the contrary). As Carl Linden has observed, "the price of [Voroshilov's] support [concerning Cuba] seemed evident in his treatment of anti-Stalinism as a dead issue for Soviet politics." (Carl Linden, "Khrushchev and the Party Battle," *Problems of Communism*, XII, May-June 1964, p. 32.)

3. The original Soviet reference to this petition appeared in a speech by Central Committee secretary Ilychev on December 17 (published in *Pravda* on December 22, 1962). The quotation above is from Ralph Blum, "Freeze and Thaw: The Artist in Soviet Russia," Part III, *The New Yorker*, XII, Sept. 11, 1965, p. 168.

4. Priscilla Johnson, *Khrushchev and the Arts*, p. 7.

5. The plenum approved Khrushchev's plans for a functional split in party and equivalent state organs and his proposals for changes in the top state economic bodies. But only two leaders strongly endorsed the reorganization, Gennaidy Voronov and Nikolai Podgorny; to the latter, incidentally, fell the task two years later of supervising the dissolution of the entire structure.

6. "If the party could no longer aspire to transform society at

will, it had to make itself useful to society; if its officials were not to be looked upon increasingly as phrase-mongering parasites, they had to prove themselves effective animators of economic progress. . . . The wheel had indeed come full circle: instead of changing the structure of society in accordance with the ideas of the party, the structure of the party was not to be changed in accordance with the supposed needs of society!" (Richard Lowenthal, "The Revolution Withers Away," *Problems of Communism*, XIV, January-February 1965, p. 16.)

7. Eisenhower, *Waging Peace*, p. 404.

8. *Newsweek*, 53, June 8, 1959, p. 33.

9. Leon Volkov, " 'Shadow Man' From Russia," *Newsweek*, 54, July 13, 1959, pp. 17–19.

10. *Time*, 74, July 13, 1959, pp. 10–13.

11. *Ibid.*

12. *Newsweek*, 53, June 8, 1959, p. 33.

13. Volkov, pp. 17–19.

14. See Robert Conquest, *Power and Policy in the U.S.S.R.* (London, 1962), pp. 79–111, 297; also Linden, *Khrushchev and the Soviet Leadership*, especially pp. 236–237.

15. Ye. Bugayev in *Pravda*, December 26, 1962.

16. V. Stepanov in *Izvestia*, February 8, 1963.

17. F. Petrenko in *Partinaya Zhizn*, No. 2, 1963.

18. Ye. Ligachev in *Ekonomicheskaya Gazeta*, January 26, 1963, pp. 3–4.

19. From the central press after the decision had been made to disband the reorganization: "Genuinely creative searching for new and better organizational forms has nothing in common with continual reorganizations. . . . Experience has not confirmed the timeliness and advisability of this reorganization, which was carried out without proper preparation, in an atmosphere of unjustified haste, and without weighing all its consequences." (*Pravda*, November 18, 1964.) "There is nothing more harmful for the cause than constant reorganizations which unjustifiably divert the efforts and attention of cadres and do not permit them to concentrate on the essence of the matter and conduct planned and fruitful work. . . . Lenin resolutely condemned 'those who

love to reorganize in every way' and considered these unending reorganizations a real disaster." (*Izvestia*, November 19, 1964.)

20. The statutes for the commission were published by *Pravda* on January 18; Carl Linden has suggested that they gave the new organ fewer real powers over party officials than Khrushchev seems initially to have wanted. Thus—as a purge instrument, controlled by Khrushchev's protege, Alexander Shelepin, the former head of the KGB—the commission may have lost some of its teeth. In any event, fear of the commission as a possible base of power, and potential instrument of terror, was surely one of the reasons it was transformed into a lesser body in December 1965.

21. As a result of administrative reshuffling (and, perhaps, bureaucratic disputes) four state committees established as a result of the November plenum were subsequently dissolved by official decree. See the invalidation of the ukase of January 21, 1963 in *Vedomosti Verkhnovo Soveta S.S.S.R.*, February 22, 1963, p. 139.

22. Johnson, p. 16.

23. *Pravda*, Feb. 28, 1963.

24. Kozlov, *Leningradskaya Pravda*, Feb. 27, 1963.

25. *Pravda*, March 10, 1963.

26. *Ibid.*, March 16, 1963.

27. While the original announcement of the creation of the Supreme National Economic Council did not refer to the Central Committee, Khrushchev, in his initial remarks on the subject on April 24, referred explicitly to the subordination of the council to both the Central Committee and the government (in that order).

28. Khrushchev told a conference of industrial workers that the defense industries, under Ustinov, had not performed as well as they should have: "The defense industry," he observed, "is coping successfully with creating and producing modern weapons," but it should have carried out its tasks "more successfully and at lower cost." (Moscow Domestic Service, April 26, 1963.)

29. Ustinov, by virtue of his position as First Deputy Premier, and according to past practices, should have been promoted to the Presidium at the June plenum. But Khrushchev did not

promote him, and for the remainder of Khrushchev's reign, Usti-nov seems for the most part to have been ignored. In the fall of 1965, the Supreme Council was dissolved, as were the regional economic councils (*sovnarkhozi*), in a reshuffling which empha-sized the recentralization of economic administration in the Mos-cow ministries. It would appear that the creation of the Supreme Council in 1963 had been considered by some of Khrushchev's unhappy colleagues (including Kosygin) simply as a stopgap measure intended to bring a measure of order to the existing administrative chaos. In any event, Ustinov finally received his promotion to the Presidium, as a candidate member, and to the Secretariat as well, but *after* Khrushchev had been removed from office.

30. Khrushchev, addressing the plenum on November 19, 1962, had declared that "in order to carry to its logical conclu-sion the responsibility of the republics for the management of the national economy and its planning, it is *necessary* to make plan-ning and the implementation of plans *fully* the tasks of the re-publics, their Gosplans and their regional economic councils." (Emphasis supplied.)

31. "This question," Khrushchev told the plenum in his speech on November 19, "deserves to be discussed again at the next plenum of the Central Committee of the CPSU. . . ." In late April, after Khrushchev had reasserted his powers and had begun to reassert his program, he again called for a plenum on the chemical industry, stating at the time that "many of our eco-nomic and *party leaders at the center,* as well as those on the spot, have so far not realized chemistry's progressive role, and the enormous economic effectiveness of chemistry for the national economy." (Emphasis supplied.) (Moscow Domestic Service, April 26, 1963.)

32. Moscow Domestic Service, December 12, 1962.

33. The Soviets were not seeking to mollify the Chinese through this affront to the Yugoslavs. Had they wished to do so the obvious place for such an effort was in the CPSU's letter to the Chinese Party of March 30, 1963. But this letter—dispatched only a little over a week before the publication of the May Day

slogans—had explicitly reiterated the view that Belgrade was building socialism.

34. *Pravda*, April 4, 1963.

35. Ponomarev was the most outspoken in this regard. He asserted in *Pravda* on November 18, 1962, that "revisionism" was the "main danger" and that its "fullest expression" could be found in Yugoslavia. During the same period, Khrushchev, writing in the November 1962 issue of *Problems of Peace and Socialism*, deliberately ignored Yugoslavia and stressed the dangers of "dogmatism" (a Chinese sin) as the potential "main danger."

36. Kozlov attended a public reception in Moscow on April 10. His illness was officially revealed in a brief announcement in *Pravda* on May 4 (after he had failed to show up for the May Day celebrations). *Le Monde* of May 26, 1963, gave April 11 as the date Kozlov was stricken (as cited by Priscilla Johnson, *op. cit.*, p. 46).

37. Khrushchev's speech to the Supreme Soviet on December 12, in which he dealt at great length with the Cuban crisis (Moscow Domestic Service, December 12, 1962).

38. *Pravda*, January 1, 1963.

39. *Ibid.*, January 17, 1963.

40. *Ibid.*, January 21, 1963.

41. Khrushchev vehemently attacked the Chinese and Albanians in his speech of December 12; *Pravda* on December 16 published the resolution of the French Communist Party which asserted that "dogmatism" was the main danger within the international communist movement; *Pravda* on December 21 claimed that "communists of all continents" recognized that "dogmatism" had become a "more and more serious danger"; and the same paper on January 7 published a long editorial which warned of the dangers of a split in the socialist camp. Then suddenly, in his speech in Berlin on January 16, Khrushchev called for a cessation of all Sino-Soviet polemics, and *Pravda* on February 10 suggested that the danger of a split had been exaggerated. It has been speculated that this change of line—accompanied by the pronounced hardening of tone toward the West—came in part as a result of pressures from conservative party figures, such as Koz-

lov and Suslov, who—while certainly not pro-Chinese—might have favored a damping down of the campaign against China, as, indeed, the leadership did in the aftermath of Khrushchev's removal.

42. The Soviet view of this collapse can be found in *International Affairs* (Moscow), No. 3, March 1963, pp. 44–45.

43. To be sure, the hardening of the Soviet line was not independent of concurrent developments in the West: the U.S.-British understanding on the Multilateral Force (after the Skybolt decision); De Gaulle's statement on January 14 about West German rights to nuclear weapons; and the signing of the Franco-German treaty by De Gaulle and Konrad Adenauer on January 22. At a minimum, these events would have encouraged the conservatives in the Soviet party to persist with an anti-detente position.

44. *Izvestia,* January 20, 1963; *Komsomolskaya Pravda,* January 20, 1963.

45. Johnson, p. 18.

46. For a full account of the Ehrenburg story, see *ibid.,* pp. 18, 19, 22–26, 65, 66.

47. *Pravda,* February 8, 1963.

48. TASS statement, *Pravda,* February 12, 1963.

49. *Pravda,* February 23, 1963.

50. Kozlov, *op. cit.*; Brezhnev, *Vechernyaya Moskva,* February 27, 1963. Kozlov in his speech was optimistic about internal prospects and avoided specific references to military spending. He took a distinctly dim view of the international scene because of the "insane" policies of the "imperialist warmongers" and was tough concerning the Berlin issue. He referred to the U.S.S.R.'s "vital national interests" in the context of the nuclear armament of West Germany and was the only civilian leader to do so in public. Brezhnev, on the other hand, was less sanguine about domestic economic prospects and specifically noted the adverse effects flowing from the necessary diversion of resources into defense needs. Further, while Kozlov was calling attention to the "unprecedented arms race," Brezhnev noted that the outlook for world peace was improving. Finally, he attributed the preserva-

tion of peace during the Cuban crisis directly to "Comrade Khrushchev" and the Central Committee, whereas Kozlov gave credit in this regard only to the Soviet government.

51. *Pravda*, April 10, 1963.

52. *Kommunist*, No. 7, April 16, 1963.

53. In fairly rapid order, beginning in early May, 1963: Khrushchev wrote to the President and—though otherwise rude and discouraging—agreed to the convening of U.S.-U.K.-Soviet talks on the matter of a test ban (see Arthur M. Schlesinger, Jr., *A Thousand Days* [Boston, 1965], p. 898); Soviet Ambassador Dobrynin talked to Secretary Dean Rusk in Washington and gave him a memorandum on disarmament; the U.S. suddenly canceled three scheduled underground nuclear tests in Nevada; Prime Minister Macmillan said that Khrushchev had given him and President Kennedy some hope for a test ban; and the President announced that Khrushchev had agreed to three-power talks on a test ban in Moscow in the near future. (See *The New York Times* of May 12, 14, 29, and June 11, 1963.)

54. *Pravda*, May 19, 1963.

55. *Neues Deutschland*, May 31, 1963.

56. An article in *Pravda* of February 13 concerning the publication of earlier volumes in the Khrushchev series had praised Khrushchev and his policies with noticeable restraint.

57. The substance of this announcement, apparently the first publicized decision of the new council, contrasted rather sharply with *Pravda*'s emphasis (on March 16) on the council's responsibilities for such matters as the introduction of new machinery into industry and the strengthening of "state discipline"; *Pravda* had not referred to the council's duties concerning consumer goods production at all.

58. Moscow Domestic Service, April 26, 1963.

59. Kozlov, speaking in Leningrad on February 26, had called for the investment of "huge funds" in the construction of new machine building enterprises. Khrushchev said on April 24 that it was "considerably more profitable" to invest in new equipment rather than new factories. Placing new equipment in existing plants, he claimed, would facilitate a transfer to two-shift

work and would bring twice the return per ruble of investment.

60. See *Ekonomicheskaya Gazeta*, April 20, 1963.

61. For example, the publication in *Pravda* on May 12 of an interview given by the liberal spokesman (and editor of *Novy Mir*) Alexander Tvardovsky, to UPI Moscow correspondent, Henry Shapiro, suggested by virtue of its "oblique support of writers who had been under fire" that "persons high in the party indeed were anxious to send out word inside the U.S.S.R. that the campaign was now to ease off a little." (Johnson, p. 49.)

62. See *ibid.*, pp. 38, 44.

63. For a full account of this unusual plenum see *ibid.*, pp. 54–60.

5. The Melancholy Recovery

THE IDEOLOGICAL PLENUM of the Central Committee in June 1963 confirmed Khrushchev's political comeback. Partly through the medium of Khrushchev's own remarks, the plenum rejected the Kozlovian line concerning culture and Stalin which had dominated during the previous winter and spring. It also reasserted Khrushchev's traditional interest in and emphasis on the needs of the Soviet consumer and the Soviet economy. Thus the liberal writers once again appeared in print and anti-Stalinism regained respectability, and thus economic discussion once more revolved around the schemes of the First Secretary. But Khrushchev seemed in other ways to be butting his head against a wall of indifference and opposition: conservative authors continued to indicate their unhappiness and to press their illiberal cause, and economic traditionalists and the military remained unreconstructed and unconvinced by Khrushchev's call for new ways to slice the nation's economic pie. More and more, it seemed, Khrushchev's recovery from the political illness which had beset him in the wake of Cuba was only a partial one.

Even before the June plenum, in order to refurbish his own political image and to restore Khrushchevism to the forefront of party consciousness, Khrushchev had moved to correct the conservative line on the arts and on Stalinism laid down in part by himself, under duress, the previous winter. Thus, in mid-April, he suspended direct and virulent attacks on the intellectuals, though he did not at the time deal directly with the issue of Stalinism. But then, in mid-June, when he spoke to the Central Committee plenum, he indicated a return to his old line toward both culture and the cult.[1] He did this indirectly, by paying relatively little attention to ideology, though the plenum had been called specifically to consider this topic; by emphasizing instead his primary concern with the national economy; and by suspending the jamming of most Western radio broadcasts directed to the Soviet Union, at a time when some other plenum speakers were decrying any form of so-called ideological coexistence. He also signaled the return to old standards directly, principally by abandoning the apologetics and the deference to Stalin so conspicuous in his previous remarks on the subject in March;[2] by emphasizing instead the grievous nature of Stalin's crimes; and by defending his decision, in the face of strong opposition, to open the whole issue for discussion at the 20th Party Congress in 1956.

Khrushchev, in addition, sought to defend his own record under Stalin, using for this purpose the device of a personal spokesman, a tactic which permitted him—though transparently—to maintain a pretence of modesty. Obviously speaking for his father-in-law, *Izvestia* editor Adzhubei told his colleagues at the plenum that, even in 1937, Khrushchev had tried to defend Marxist-Leninist purity against the assaults of Stalin. He quoted from remarks made by Khrushchev at the time—remarks which were, in fact, essentially meaningless in the context of their purported significance—to refute the views of "those writers who assert that [during] the period of the cult of Stalin's personality . . . there were no forces in the party which defended truly Leninist principles. . . ." [3]

Adzhubei also had some things to say, in effect, about Khrushchev's critics and those party leaders who had been responsible for the convocation of a plenum on ideology in the first place.

> Some people are inclined to divide party work into the purely economic and the purely ideological. It will seem to [them] that if the party struggles . . . to develop new branches of industry and to lift agriculture, it is engaging in purely economic problems, to the detriment of theory. . . . As for the sorry theoreticians who engage [only] in writing . . . pompous theoretical works on abstract themes—such theoreticians seem important only to themselves. [4]

Khrushchev's reassertion of his own views on Stalin and of his relatively permissive attitude toward the writers of (moderate) dissent was soon echoed by Podgorny, [5] and then—to make matters unmistakably clear—was again emphasized by Khrushchev himself in late July. "No one," he protested, "can whiten these black deeds of the period of the cult of personality. . . . Every Soviet person, every Communist, knows that the banner certain people wish to raise [in defense of Stalin] is covered with the blood of revolutionaries, of Communists, of honest working people of the Soviet Union." [6]

Khrushchev went out of his way in August to assure Soviet writers that they need no longer fear a neo-Stalinist revival. In an uncharacteristically effective and original gesture (perhaps inspired by Adzhubei, an opportunist who nonetheless had modernist tastes), he invited a number of Western European novelists and the Soviet poet, Alexander Tvardovsky, editor of the liberal literary magazine, *Novy Mir,* to visit him at his vacation spot in Gagra. There Khrushchev asked Tvardovsky to read aloud his new and vigorously anti-Stalinist poem, "Terkin in the Other World." [7] The subsequent publication of this lengthy work in *Izvestia,* even before it appeared as scheduled in *Novy Mir,* signified to the public at large that respectability now lay again with those who condemned Stalin rather than with those who, even indirectly, sought to defend him. [8]

It was during this same period that Ilya Ehrenburg made some interesting remarks to a number of Western writers attending a conference on the novel held in Leningrad in July.

> The right to the existence of experiments in literature cannot be denied. [But], dear guests, you must understand that we are living in the first century of the socialist society and that we have more enemies than we need. . . . Our writers sometimes write bad novels, not because they are bound to the socialist ideology, but because the Lord God did not give them talent. We never said that under socialism there would be no poor talent. We said that there would be no exploiters—we have none—but there are plenty of untalented writers. [9]

The poet Yevtushenko reappeared on the literary scene in September with a series of poems which, if politically ambiguous, nonetheless failed to apologize for his earlier sins. In October, Tvardovsky, in an editorial note in *Novy Mir,* promised his readers that a host of liberal authors were scheduled to appear in future editions of his magazine, including Ehrenburg, Alexander Solzhenitsyn, Nekrasov, and

Vasiliy Aksenov. In November, the controversial poet Andrei Voznesensky, who had had a face-to-face set-to with Khrushchev in March, published in the journal *Znamya;* according to Priscilla Johnson, his verses were as full of "formal innovation" and as "irreverent" as ever. And other liberal poets and writers—even including the heavily censured Viktor Nekrasov—now appeared, if not with frequency, at least with sufficient regularity to imply a return to the pre-Kozlovian status quo.[10]

Sometime during the summer, Khrushchev began very gradually to encourage a campaign to correct his own remarks of March 8 concerning the party's alleged ignorance of Stalin's misdeeds. Partly, perhaps, as a followup to Adzhubei's protestations in June to the effect that Khrushchev had sought to resist Stalin in 1937, the journal *Voprosy Istori KPSS* (Problems of CPSU History) in July reviewed a work on party military history and concluded that the book demonstrated that in Stalin's time "many military Communists . . . spoke out against the unjustified repressions."[11] A Moscow radio broadcast in mid-September described a clash said to have taken place between Stalin and a party official named I. M. Vareykis, who had had the temerity to question the arrest of Marshal Mikhail Tukhachevsky and who was therefore himself arrested only a few days later.[12] *Izvestia* joined the parade in November with a tribute to an old Komsomol leader, A. V. Kosarev, who had "spoken in defense of his arrested colleagues whenever he could" and who had frequently expressed suspicion as to why "such a number of enemies had suddenly appeared in our country."[13]

Pravda brought the point of much of this into the open by returning in March to the sensitive question of what Khrushchev had been doing during the Stalinist era.[14] A group of revolutionary veterans in Lvov, *Pravda* claimed, had recently "recalled with gratitude that N. S. Khrushchev, during his stay in the Ukraine, even under the conditions of the Stalin personality cult, did everything to save the old cadres of the Western Ukrainian Communist Party." This tribute to Khrushchev of course called implicit attention to the contrast between Khrushchev's allegedly heroic actions and the nefarious activities of such men as Beria, Molotov, and Malenkov, who had been accused by Khrushchev (as, for example, at the 22nd Party Congress in 1961) not only of knowledge of Stalin's crimes but also of complicity in them.

This campaign reached a climax (or, indeed, an anti-climax) of sorts in May when, in a review in *Izvestia* of a new novel, *Soldiers Are Not Born*, fictional treatment of Stalin was given official sanction.

> The scene [in the novel] of Serpilin's meeting with Sta-lin is described with special force. Summoned to Mos-cow, Serpilin goes to Stalin to tell him honestly and frankly what has been incessantly tormenting him as a Communist throughout the war years, to tell him about 1937. . . . But in the course of the conversation, Serpilin suddenly realizes—*he reads this in Stalin's eyes*—that all these things had not been mistakes, but crimes, and that there was no one to complain to! (Emphasis supplied.)[15]

That the Khrushchev line on literature had been recon-firmed, and that there was an open and officially endorsed renewal of the campaign against Stalin, did not by any means silence the literary conservatives. The liberal writers remained the subjects of tendentious critiques and sharp re-bukes in certain conservatively inclined literary magazines. Any form of innovation was instantly denounced,[16] as were the so-called sin of "de-heroization" (portraying the protag-onist in other than a heroic, "positive" light) and the trend toward something labeled as "universal forgiveness" (portraying the villains in other than a totally negative light).[17] Even Solzhenitsyn—by now an international literary hero—continued to be abused because he dared to portray life in a realistic way.[18]

Matters, however, never really progressed very much beyond this uncertain balance between a somewhat ambiguous official campaign and a constricted, though nonetheless strident, countercampaign. The liberal writers, though published and no longer subject to harassment or punishment, remained relatively cautious, either because they sensed the need to avoid provocations, or because they were subjected to one or another form of prophylactic pressure. The conservatives were on the defensive and for the most part were excluded from making the sort of hard-line pronouncements in the central press that they had been able to during the previous winter. They were successful, nonetheless, in making their presence felt and in blatantly advertising their neo-Stalinist views in the pages of their own journals.

Khrushchev almost certainly wished to carry his anti-Stalinist campaign further. He no doubt wished, in fact, to begin again where he had been impelled to leave off in the fall of 1962, using anti-Stalinism as a weapon against his domestic opponents. Indeed, the posthumous rehabilitation of the economist N. A. Vozhnesensky in July had for a time looked as if it might be the beginning of a campaign against Suslov, who in 1952 had been none other than the first person publicly to condemn Vozhnesensky's alleged economic heresies.[19] But nothing had come of this, and no other similar signs of impending purge were forthcoming.

Khrushchev did not again show any strong inclination to use anti-Stalinism as a direct instrument of political warfare. His interest in its possible future use was not likely to be doubted, however, not only because of the continued appearance in the press of anti-Stalinist material, but also because of his reversion to the theme that he and only a few of his contemporaries—none of whom had managed to survive —had resisted Stalin even in the darkest days of purge and terror. The principal implication of this was, of course, that most of the other senior leaders were vulnerable to charges of having been sinners under Stalin (which, though together with Khrushchev, they had been).

All in all, during the remainder of 1963 and for the first nine months of 1964, both the cultural scene in general and the anti-Stalinist campaign in particular exhibited few signs of real movement. Khrushchev had clearly been able to correct the wrongs of the Kozlovian consolidation of early 1963, but he had been unable to do much more than that. He was blocked from proceeding any further, apparently in part by his own uncertainties and fears, and by his own disinclination to surrender any real party control over maverick intellectuals. But, more important, he also seems to have been stymied by the conservative establishment itself and by his own wary colleagues. The signs of the time (not to mention those of the past) were that Khrushchev had wished, though in vain, to wind up his anti-Stalinist movement with the dismissal of some of his colleagues and with some form of definitive statement for posterity concerning the evils of Stalin and his times. In this way, apparently, he had sought to insure for himself a permanent niche in the gallery of "positive" Soviet heroes.

It was wholly in character for Khrushchev in the summer of 1963 to seize on some great (and unrealistic) scheme to symbolize both his return to preeminence and his ability to propel Soviet society and the Soviet economy forward on a grand scale. In 1957 and 1958, in the midst of a wave of optimism which had swept over the Soviet leadership, Khrushchev had tried to advance the cause of Soviet Communism by promising that the U.S.S.R. would soon catch and even surpass the United States in the production of such consumer products as meat, milk, and butter. Surely here—however bizarre—was a goal worthy of the burgeoning socialist society, one to dazzle the home folk and dismay the capitalist enemy. Early, in 1954, even before his assumption of dominant power, Khrushchev had turned the nation's attention to agriculture by inaugurating a project for the settlement and exploitation of the vast new agricultural lands (the Virgin Lands) in Western Siberia and Kazakhstan. Here too was a great scheme to capture the imagination of the long-neglected Soviet consumer.

And so it went, the sweeping promises, the grandiose schemes, the mammoth projects, and the flamboyant Khrushchev style—not just in agriculture, but also in housing, in chemicals, in strategic rockets, and in space. The Soviet economy, large but not limitless and managed with much waste and inefficiency, simply could not provide Khrushchev with the means to satisfy his many and ambitious ends. But Khrushchev—in addition to a mighty but only partly successful effort to hold down military spending—grasped at straws (so called "hidden reserves" in the economy) and had boundless faith in his own energies and abilities. He was determined to transform the economy into an engine of gross and various accomplishment, capable of improving the conditions of the people at large and, simultaneously, of providing the wherewithal, both military and economic, for the U.S.S.R's great competition with the West.

Then, in 1963, in the aftermath of Cuba and the challenge to his position, Khrushchev rediscovered the backward Soviet chemical industry and proclaimed the need to expand dramatically the output of chemical fertilizers. The magic figure was to be 100 million tons of annual production by 1970. This is what Khrushchev initially demanded, and this, apparently, was to have been his new battle cry. Somehow, it seemed more than ordinarily appropriate. After years of emphasis on corn and meat, the cosmos above and the perfect society below, Khrushchev now found himself in the position of, in effect, taking it all back. He was starting again, at the beginning, trying to persuade the party and the managers and, indeed, the society as a whole, that life's most important and glorious task now lay in the production of simple nutrients for the soil.

Khrushchev first referred to his fertilizer goal privately, in a note to the CPSU Presidium in July 1963. "For all agriculture," he wrote, "86 million tons of fertilizer are required, and taking into consideration the needs of other branches of the national economy, we must produce 100 million tons of mineral fertilizers." [20] During the same month, in remarks to U.S. Secretary of Agriculture Orville Freeman—which were not published until the following year—he repeated the figure and revealed the way in which the goal was to be achieved: "Now we will reduce expenditures on defense and direct this money also to the production of mineral fertilizers." [21]

Khrushchev, taking his campaign to the people, referred to the 100-million-ton target figure in speeches given during a farm tour in mid-September, and the Soviet press mentioned the figure several times in October and early November.[22] *Pravda* mentioned it on November 14, roughly a month before the convocation of the plenum specifically scheduled to discuss Khrushchev's program for the Soviet chemical industry. But, obviously, all was not well with Khrushchev's campaign, and this it turned out, was to be the last time the magic figure appeared in the press.

Suddenly, on November 17, *Pravda* published a letter signed by seven agricultural experts who expressed serious doubts about Khrushchev's ambitious fertilizer goal. The letter did not, of course, name the First Secretary or suggest specifically that Khrushchev's target figure was grandiose. But it explicitly attacked a call for 86 million tons, claiming that even this quantity would be in excess of actual needs if supplies were properly used. In their comments appended to the letter, the editors of *Pravda* seemed favorably impressed. Khrushchev's demand for 100 million tons had evidently been rejected! Or it had all, somehow, simply been a 100 million-ton misunderstanding!

On December 9, Khrushchev confirmed his own defeat when he delivered a report to the Central Committee pithily entitled, "The Accelerated Development of the Chemical Industry Is a Major Condition for an Upsurge of Agriculture Production and a Rise in the Well-Being of the People." [23] The report laid out Khrushchev's massive new program for the Soviet chemical industry, calling for a total capital investment in the period 1963–1970 of some 42 billion rubles.[24] The gross output of the major branches of the industry was planned to grow some 200–300 percent by 1970; herbicide and pesticide production was scheduled to grow during the same period some 650 percent, and chemical fibres by 340 percent. But the production of mineral fertilizers, while planned to increase some 250–300 percent, was no longer to reach 100 million tons in 1970. Far from it—the new figure specified only some 70–80 million tons.

Despite this rather impressive paring down of Khrushchev's original fertilizer target, the chemical program as a whole remained ambitious and demanding. It would, in fact, according to Khrushchev, impose a burden on other as yet unspecified sectors of the economy. "It may be," Khrushchev told the plenum, "that to accomplish this [program] we will have to slow down temporarily the growth of certain other branches of industry." [25]

Later in December, at the annual session of the Supreme

Soviet called to consider the next year's state budget, Khrushchev, forced to trim his own goals, gained a measure of revenge on those interests which had surely been among those opposing the high fertilizer figure. The existing targets for the steel industry for 1970 were cut back some 6–8 million tons (to 89 million tons), the defense budget for 1964 was lowered by some 600 million rubles, and Khrushchev announced that the state was contemplating a further reduction in the manpower strength of the armed forces.[26] In themselves, these decreases were not large enough to finance the chemical program, but Khrushchev probably intended them to indicate the economic sectors most likely to bear the burden of further cuts.

Predictably, the military—already restive over the partial test ban treaty—was especially unhappy about Khrushchev's defense budget and his announced desire to reduce the size of the armed forces. In the problem as, in effect, stated by the First Secretary, guns vs. fertilizer (and then, after fertilizer, presumably butter), the military establishment could favor only the former. "I do not know how it is in your country," Khrushchev told an Egyptian audience in mid-May 1964, "but my esteemed friend the President [Nasser] would be able to tell me whether a military person ever tells him: 'Do not give us any more weapons, there are enough of them!' " [27]

With very few exceptions following the December plenum, the marshals deliberately avoided any references to a possible troop cut.[28] They referred, though infrequently, to the reduction in the defense budget, but indicated their opposition indirectly by stressing the growth of defense budgets and the buildup of conventional forces in the West. They also alluded to the U.S.S.R.'s allegedly strong need for conventional forces (*e.g.*, the ground forces) as well as the advanced elements so favored by Khrushchev (*e.g.*, the strategic rocket troops). As put in December 1963 by Marshal Vasily Chuikov: "In modern conditions, the ground forces continue to be not only an essential but also a most important integral part of the armed forces." [29] And, apparently in order to supplement this kind of oblique opposition to any troop cuts, Marshal Malinovsky, the defense minister, suggested in April that it was the party's responsibility to consult military leaders on questions involving national security. He claimed that, concerning any "urgent problems of military development," the Central Committee and the Presidium make detailed studies and "consult leading military cadres [before] a concrete decision is reached." [30]

As had been apparent for some time in the military press, the military's concept of what might constitute "urgent problems of military development" was considerably broader than many in the party would be likely to wish to admit.[31] The military, for example, did not view the formulation of economic policy as something which belonged solely within the province of the party politicians and the government economists. When Khrushchev sought to divert funds from defense and to reallocate them to the chemical industry, or even when he sought to transfer funds from heavy industry (especially the metallurgical industries) for the sake of one or another of his pet programs, the military was understandably concerned and, to the extent possible, resisted. The priority development of metals, a millitary spokesman asserted, for example, is the "fundament of all industry." [32]

Sympathy with this point of view also was expressed at times by top civilian leaders. Economic czar Ustinov, the former chief of military production, speaking in November 1963 to a conference of trade union officials, specified an order of economic development priorities which echoed that spelled out the previous spring during a high point of conservative influence on national economic policy.[33] Ustinov called for a "sharp upsurge" of chemistry, power, machine building, radio electronics, and special metallurgy. Then—apparently as a distinctly secondary project—he asked for the development at only "rapid rates" of industrial branches whose products would facilitate an increase in crop yields, *e.g.*, fertilizers.[34]

Presumably as a consequence of one form or another of resistance to his chemical program—and because, in fact, some of his program needed further spelling out—Khrushchev convened a Central Committee plenum on agriculture in February 1964. In his major address to this meeting, he called for intensified agriculture (higher yields, more specialization) and vigorously defended his chemical industry plans, very much as if they had been under severe attack. He referred to the critics and skeptics—who almost certainly included Ustinov and Kosygin—as "hidebound dogmatists."[35] He insisted that everyone should understand that the chemical program was not simply a "fad," that it had not been instituted as the result of some sort of "craze," and that the kind of footdragging which planning officials had been guilty of since 1958—treating the problem as if it were "secondary"—could no longer be tolerated.

At the same time, seemingly giving a little to some of his opponents, Khrushchev promised that his plans would in no way harm the military or injure the future growth of the economy as a whole. The chemical industry, he claimed, represented "an excellent synthesis of the interests of the state and people in the development of heavy industry and the concern of the Soviet people for a rapid increase in the output of consumer goods." Nevertheless, while the "party will continue to display concern for the development of heavy industry . . . it has never considered this a goal in itself." There should no longer be any "counterposing of Group A and Group B [heavy and light industry]." [36]

In late February, within weeks of the end of the plenum, Khrushchev summoned a Central Committee conference to discuss the implementation of the plenum's decisions. His speech to this gathering placed primary emphasis on the need for material incentives in agriculture.[37] He did not repeat the proposals of a recent provocative article in *Kommunist,* which, *inter alia,* had advocated a guaranteed annual wage for collective farmers, but he did place great stress on the issue of incentives as a whole.[38] "One can economize on everything," he said, "but one cannot compromise on the material stimulus." But the implications of this revealing remark—the imposition of an inflexible priority for higher payments to the peasants—were apparently too bold and controversial; *Pravda,* in belatedly publishing the full text of this speech, carefully excised the entire passage.[39]

It seems likely that Khrushchev had been unable to say all that he had wanted to at these February meetings. Accordingly, and to indicate the direction he was heading without necessarily committing himself to it, he resorted to the use of a spokesman to come forward with his more radical proposals. Thus *Pravda* in late February ran a two-part article by the economist, Anushavan Arzumanyan, under the title, "Urgent Problems of Developing Our Economy." [40] It was the most radical economic platform yet advanced in a party publication and, though still somewhat disguised by euphemisms and appeals to doctrine, the piece as a whole fairly rang with proposals for fundamental change.

Arzumanyan began his piece by suggesting that a part of the Leninist scriptures should be amended to take account of the policies of Khrushchev. The First Secretary's program for the development of the chemical program, he wrote, should be accorded "the same importance Lenin attributed to the country's electrification." It was time for a change, and a big one at that:

> The question arises: If socialism is not production for the sake of consumption by the popular masses, what is the purpose of socialist production? . . . for the sake of profit? . . . for the sake of production? Of course not. The party has come forward against the dogmatic interpretation of the law of the preferential growth of the means of production. . . . The task of comprehensively developing the output of consumer goods is extremely urgent and important. . . . The answer to the question of how much the first category [heavy industry] can allocate to the second [light industry] . . . depends on specific historical conditions. . . . Therefore, *the proportions between the first and second are changeable.* (Emphasis supplied.)

Thus Arzumanyan, almost certainly speaking for Khrushchev, sought to repeal the law of preferential growth for heavy industry. Khrushchev had long sought, in effect, to do this himself, but had never been able to do so in public.[41] Now it appeared as if the stage had finally been set, and that Khrushchev would make it all official at the next plenum of the Central Committee. Such, at any rate, seemed to be a necessary doctrinal and political precursor to any truly ambitious amendment of the nation's system of allocational priorities. Existing theology and its advocates seemed to require a direct refutation and a direct rebuke before further progress could be made.

"The decisions of the September 1953 Central Committee Plenum, the 20th Party Congress, and subsequent plenums on agriculture," *Kommunist* had observed the previous fall in an unusually frank commentary, "have been implemented in a circumstance of implacable struggle by the party against conservatives and dogmatists." [42] These forces (not otherwise identified), which had long used the allegedly immutable priority of investment in heavy industry as a means to hinder investment in agriculture, were now, at long last, to receive a belated comeuppance. Or so it seemed.

But those who thereafter looked for some form of definitive followup to Azumanyan's brave statement were, as it turned out, completely disappointed. Neither the party press nor Khrushchev himself refuted Arzumayan's theses, nor, however,—and this, in the end, counted for more—did they confirm them. The closest Khrushchev seems to have come to it (except for a statement in September, just before his ouster) was in a speech to the Supreme Soviet in July, but his remarks then were a far cry from those expected. "Here I should say, comrades," Khrushchev remarked, mildly, "that as yet not all of our leaders have really understood the importance of constantly increasing the output of consumer goods. . . . The possibility has now appeared for allocating more funds for the development of the production of consumer goods." [43]

Another Khrushchevian campaign of this period met a similar fate. In late February *Izvestia* published a letter entitled, "The Labor Passport Is the Identity of the U.S.S.R. Citizen," to which the editors attached "great importance." [44] The writers, allegedly a deputy of the Supreme Soviet and two steelworkers from Donetsk, advocated the adoption by the government of a "labor passport" on which would appear, among other things, a man's work record and evaluations of his performance on the job. The passport would be designed to assist the regime in spotting (and punishing) "loafers and parasites" and would, hopefully, help to solve the problem of excess labor mobility. *Izvestia* asked its readers for comments. Letters apparently then began to pour into Moscow, and almost all of them seemed to be enthusiastic. *Pravda, Selskaya Zhizn,* and even provincial papers began to run series of such communications.[45] Khrushchev himself, in a speech delivered only two days after the initial proposal, said that he considered the idea to be "correct," asserted that he "fully supported it," and added that "each person should have such a passport." [46] Despite this firm endorsement and the elaborate support for the proposal in the press, the plan came, in the end, to naught. No new system of labor passports was ever instituted.

Khrushchev's program for the chemical industry and the consumer had been launched in December amidst considerable anxiety and uncertainty about the economy. The 1963 harvest had been almost disastrous; grain production totaled an estimated 92 million tons, some 27 millions below the previous high of 1958, and total gross farm output also fell below the 1958 figure.[47] There was little the regime could do to conceal the fact or to cover up its dismay: "We need grain now, comrades," Khrushchev admitted in late September before an audience of farmers in the southern Ukraine. "Unfavorable weather conditions arose this year, and we are in a difficult position and are obliged to draw the necessary conclusions." [48] Similarly, addressing a crowd in Krasnodar during the same month, Khrushchev confessed that, "as a result of [unusually bad weather] a difficult situation formed in 1963, and we cannot harvest the quantity of grain we had counted on." Therefore, he revealed, "we had to purchase grain abroad." [49]

The gravity of the situation and its effects on the political processes were revealed by Khrushchev in an interview he granted in late October, 1963. Indicating that the CPSU Presidium had debated the matter, Khrushchev stated that there were "two paths" to follow in view of the harvest crisis: belt tightening or purchases abroad. "Some people," he said, had favored the former, which he then denounced as redolent of the "methods of Stalin and Molotov," who had not flinched at "starving the people." [50] Khrushchev, of course, decided on the latter course, and, ultimately, the U.S.S.R. bought some $800 million of Western wheat, including large quantities from the United States.

The bad 1963 harvest may have helped Khrushchev's plans in at least one respect: it demonstrated with great clarity that *something* had to be done to insure adequate agricultural production. *Kommunist* condemned the attitude still widely held that the old ways would suffice and that farm output need not be a matter of major concern:

> Unfortunately, many party and soviet leaders, flushed by successes . . . [since 1953] ceased to think about using new reserves, supposing that it was possible to continue moving production ahead by the old methods. . . . In several oblasts and republics . . . the principle of material incentives again began to be violated. . . . All this taken together led to a slackening in the tempo of growth of production in comparison with that achieved for 1953–1958, and to a serious lag . . . [with respect to] the goals of the Seven-Year Plan period.[51]

Apparently, lest past triumphs tended to obscure anyone's vision and lest Khrushchev's blaming of the weather for the 1963 performance permitted any complacency about the future, *Kommunist* also warned that in a way there really had been nothing unique about the harvest just in. On the contrary, that is the way things had been heading for several years: "The slackening in the tempo of agricultural development—during 1958 to 1962 the growth of gross [farm] product comprised only 7 percent—aroused the just alarm of the Central Committee. . . ." [52]

But while the lesson should have been unmistakable

after 1963, this did not mean that all could agree as to the precise remedies required, or even the level of investment indicated for whatever was deemed necessary. No doubt there were pet nostrums aplenty (*e.g.*, the exotic genetic theories of the Lysenkoites), and there were, in addition, a variety of competitive vested interests involved in *any* overall approach to the agriculture problem. Moreover, in terms of prospects for Khrushchev's programs, the 1963 harvest could only have added to his political difficulties. The miserable showing of the Virgin Lands was a blow to his prestige, the overall production default represented a defeat of sorts for his general agricultural policies, and the situation as a whole gave promise of assisting Khrushchev's opponents in their efforts to restrain him in the future.

In April, 1964, Khrushchev wrote yet another agricultural note to the Presidium. This one dealt with "Several Questions Connected with the Implementation of the Party's Course Toward the Intensification of Agriculture." [53] It was even more tedious than most, for it dealt entirely with the improvement of the systems used to instruct agricultural cadres, the production of animal husbandry products on an industrial basis, and the improvement of the work of the agricultural production administrations.

The Central Committee quickly approved the note and established a commission to deal with these problems. At its head was no less a personage than Nikolai Podgorny, member of both the CPSU Presidium and Secretariat. Serving under him were such luminaries as Brezhnev, Kosygin, Mikoyan, Polyansky, Voronov, and others.[54] The commission was directed in one month's time (a deadline it did not meet) to come forth with specific proposals on the industrial production of meat and poultry, the production of pork in large specialized state farms, the establishment of factories for the industrial feeding of pigs, and the development along specialized lines of state dairy farms. Thus, it almost seemed, did the Central Committee respond to the revolutionary proposals of Arzumanyan!

In July, Khrushchev did manage to gain approval for his emphasis on material incentives for farmers and for workers in various service activities (education, housing, public health, etc.).[55] The Supreme Soviet at that time decided to give pensions to farmers, on a contributory basis, and to grant outright wage increases (averaging 21 percent) to service workers. But, though this was certainly more in the spirit of Arzumanyan than the industrial feeding of pigs, Khrushchev had to admit that these measures, far from being novel, were, in fact, belated. "It was originally intended," he confessed, "to carry out [these wage raises and pension plans] . . . in 1962, but certain foreign and domestic considerations forced us to postpone them temporarily." [56] And then, in a reference to the sorry state of affairs in economic management, and with at least an implicit rebuke to those who wished to scrap some of his schemes for administrative reform (simply because they apparently had not worked!) Khrushchev seemed a great deal less than optimistic.

> In recent years, as is known, the party Central Committee and the government had been greatly concerned with questions of reorganizing the system of management of industry, construction, and agriculture. What has been done is fully justifying itself. But it would be incorrect to feel that we have done everything in this regard. . . . Lenin taught us that one need not be afraid to cast aside all that has become obsolete and burdensome, that one must not drop an undertaking that is not at first successful, but must work it out again in all its details until the desired result is achieved.

Finally, Khrushchev summed up recent times in what must have been one of the more melancholy statements of his entire career:

> Not quite three years have passed since the 22nd CPSU Congress adopted the new party program. This is not a very long period, of course. Moreover, during these three years we have not always been accompanied by favorable factors and fair winds. There have been certain difficulties of both a domestic and foreign nature. Despite this, things are going well for us. . . .

NOTES

1. *Pravda*, June 21, 1963.
2. *Ibid.*, March 10, 1963.
3. *Izvestia*, June 20, 1963.
4. *Ibid.*
5. *Pravda Ukrainy*, July 4, 1965.
6. *Pravda*, July 20, 1963.
7. *Pravda*, August 14, 1963.
8. *Izvestia*, August 18, 1963; *Novy Mir*, No. 8, 1963.
9. *Literaturnaya Gazeta*, August 13, 1963.
10. For a fuller description of the literary climate at this time and of the return of these writers to the pages of Soviet journals, see Priscilla Johnson, *Khrushchev and the Arts*, pp. 78–84.
11. *Voprosy Istori KPSS*, No. 7, 1963.
12. Moscow Domestic Service, September 18, 1963.
13. *Izvestia*, November 14, 1963.
14. *Pravda*, March 28, 1964.
15. *Izvestia*, May 30, 1964.
16. See, for example, A. Elyashevich in *Zvezda*, No. 8, 1963, pp. 185–202.
17. *E.g.*, V. Novikov, in *Znamya*, No. 9, 1963, pp. 184–187.
18. *E.g.*, V. Chalmayev, in *Oktyabr*, No. 10, 1963, pp. 215–217.
19. Vozhnesensky's contributions to Soviet economics, and his unfortunate demise as a result of Stalin's arbitrariness were discussed initially in *Voprosy Istori KPSS*, No. 6, 1963, pp. 94–98; Suslov's Stalinist assault on Vozhnesensky appeared in *Pravda*, December 24, 1962.
20. "On the Development of the Production of Mineral Fertilizers for Full Satisfaction of the Demands of Agriculture: Note to the Presidium of the Central Committee, July 12, 1963," *Stroitelstvo Kommunizma v S.S.R. i Razvitiye Selskovo Khozyaistva*

(Construction of Communism in the U.S.S.R. and the Development of Agriculture), Vol. 8 (signed to the printer on April 6, 1964), pp. 23–43.

21. "Talk with a Delegation of Agricultural Specialists of the U.S.A.," *ibid.*, p. 51.

22. See *Pravda*, October 2, 1963; *Tass*, October 9, 1963; *Izvestia*, November 13, 1963.

23. *Pravda*, December 10, 1963.

24. At the official exchange rate, this sum would approximate U.S. $47 billion. But in terms of Soviet costs, the true dollar equivalent would be well above this figure.

25. *Pravda*, December 10, 1963.

26. *Ibid.*, December 17, 1963.

27. Khrushchev, as broadcast live, Cairo Radio, May 18, 1964. This remark was heavily edited before it appeared, as follows, in the Soviet press: "I do not know how it is in your country . . . but in our country the military, in their solicitude for the strengthening of the country's defense capacity, are in no hurry to declare: Enough appropriations for these ends!" (*Pravda*, May 19, 1964.)

28. Marshal Malinovsky mentioned it in articles prepared for the Eastern European press on the occasion of Soviet Armed Forces Day (*e.g., Neues Deutschland*, February 23, 1964), but these articles were not published in Soviet media.

29. *Izvestia*, December 21, 1963.

30. *Krasnaya Zvezda*, April 17, 1964.

31. For discussions of this general problem, see Matthew P. Gallagher, "Military Manpower, a Case Study," and Thomas W. Wolfe, "Political Primacy vs. Professional Elan," both in *Problems of Communism*, Vol. XIII, No. 3, May-June, 1964, pp. 44–62.

32. I. Punanov, "The Material-Technical Base of Communism and the Strengthening of the Country's Defense Capacity," *Kommunist Vooruzhennykh sil*, No. 18, 1964.

33. See, for example, *Pravda*, March 31, 1963.

34. TASS, Novemer 1, 1963. With the single exception of

Komsomolskaya Pravda, the central (Moscow) press chose to ignore these passages in Ustinov's speech. Much of the provincial press (*e.g., Sovetskaya Estonia,* November 1, 1963) reproduced them in full.

35. *Pravda,* February 15, 1964.

36. *Ibid.*

37. *Pravda,* March 7, 1964.

38. K. Karpov in *Kommunist,* No. 2, 1964.

39. The remark appeared in a summary of the speech in *Pravda,* February 29, 1964; it was removed from the text as it appeared in the same paper on March 7, 1964.

40. *Pravda,* February 24 and 25, 1964.

41. He had, however, done so privately. In May 1961 he remarked to a number of Western correspondents at the British Trade Fair in Moscow that light and heavy industries would soon be able to grow at the same rate. See *The New York Times,* May 21, 1961.

42. *Kommunist,* No. 13, 1963, pp. 1–10.

43. *Pravda,* July 14, 1964.

44. *Izvestia,* February 26, 1964.

45. See, for example, *Pravda,* February 29, 1964, *Selskaya Zhizn,* March 31, 1964, and *Sovetskaya Moldavia,* April 2, 1964.

46. *Pravda,* March 7, 1964.

47. See Douglas Diamond, "Trends in Output, Inputs and Factor Productivity in Soviet Agriculture," in *New Directions in the Soviet Economy* (Joint Economic Committee, U.S. Congress 1966), IIB, p. 369. Also *Problems of Communism,* Vol. XIV, No. 3, May-June 1965, table p. 12.

48. *Pravda,* October 1, 1963.

49. *Ibid.,* October 2, 1963.

50. *Ibid.,* October 27, 1963.

51. *Kommunist,* No. 13, 1963, pp. 1–10.

52. *Ibid.* This article was also interesting because it revealed that the Soviet grain harvest in 1953 came to some 435 kg. per capita, which was some 106 kg. *less* than the equivalent figures for 1913!

53. *Pravda*, April 24, 1964.

54. *Ibid.*

55. *Pravda*, July 14, 1964; the relevant laws are published in *Pravda*, July 16, 1964.

56. *Pravda*, July 14, 1964.

6. Power Politics

KHRUSHCHEV, IN THE AFTERMATH of his struggle with Kozlov and his domestic opponents in the spring of 1963, was not the man he had once been. Never, in the remaining year and a half or so of his reign, did he seem able to reassert fully the powers he had once held over his colleagues and over the course of national policy as a whole. He was able to reward at least some of his closest allies with promotions; Brezhnev and Podgorny were both placed on the party Secretariat in June 1963, to serve as joint (and presumably competing) successors to the ailing Kozlov. But Khrushchev seemed quite unable to strengthen his position with a natural corollary of this promotion of his friends, a purge of his enemies.

Of course, the political environment of the time was, at best, a gloomy one. Neither the overall lack of domestic policy momentum nor the deepening sag in the performance of the economy was likely to assist the First Secretary in his efforts to regain the political summit. The near-disastrous wheat harvest of 1963 was sufficient in itself to bring about probably the gravest economic crisis in post-Stalin Soviet history.

The U.S.S.R.'s policies abroad in this period were also cause for concern. Relations with the Chinese were deteriorating at an accelerating rate, and some members of the elite no doubt began to find some comfort in the simplistic notion that this trend could be arrested, or even reversed, if Khrushchev were merely removed from office. (This notion was, in fact, tested after Khrushchev's removal, but was soon found to be sadly wanting in substance.) To be sure, relations with the West were, at the same time, improving, but many within the party were skeptical about this or opposed to it altogether. Some, certainly, were fearful that a relaxation with the West could be purchased only at the cost of a further decline in relations with the Chinese, a dilution of Soviet ideological purity, and a weakening of the U.S.S.R.'s overall international posture. In any case, the relaxation of relations with the U.S. could, by doctrinal and conventional Soviet standards, hardly be counted as a positive triumph of Soviet policy.

It is possible, of course, that these problems would have mattered less if Khrushchev had been able to overcome his vicissitudes of the previous year with greater flair and skill. His victory over the conservatives may have been, after all, as much a matter of sheer good luck, Kozlov's fortuitous illness, as anything else. Surely his image would have gained more had he been able to outwit or outplay his principal challenger instead of merely outlasting him.

Finally, in the context of Khrushchev's internal political problems, the First Secretary's relations with his nominal peers on the CPSU Presidium seem to have been modified. Khrushchev had been politically disfigured by his unsuccessful Cuban venture—itself the product of disappointment and even desperation—and had then been further scarred by his bout with Kozlov and the conservatives. All of this was surely visible, and, in the eyes of his contemporaries, helped to bring him down to life-size as a leader. None of the members of the Presidium were anxious to replace Kozlov in the lists, but together, as a group, emboldened by Khrushchev's close call the previous spring, they seem to have been more willing and able than ever to place constraints on his activities. The power and influence of the aging and, by now, notoriously fallible Khrushchev had, in fact, waned, and a measure of his charisma had left him as a consequence. The story of Khrushchev's final period in power is thus very largely a story of frustration, and, ultimately, of failure.

The return to presumably modern and forward-looking party leadership under Khrushchev following the period of presumably banal Kozlovian retrenchment in the winter and spring was seemingly hailed by *Izvestia* in early July 1963 in a gloating essay called "Against Political Twaddle." [1] The piece (in which editor Adzhubei almost certainly had a direct hand) began by condemning the sterility of old-style party leaders:

> There are still comrades among us who cannot be restrained at any meeting, who are ready to report the truisms from a course in political science to any audience and who even look upon this as some kind of political action. . . . [Such orators] will say exactly the same thing, in the same words, at a conference of advanced livestock raisers, at a rally of women volunteers, and at a gathering of a Young Pioneer detachment. Who needs this depressing revival of formalism in work with people?

And then, in words worthy of the cult of personality, and stronger even than was to be the pattern in the months ahead, the article addressed itself to the style of the First Secretary.

And how many bright generalizing images and clearly, expressively formulated conclusions, how much lofty civic passion in the speeches of N. S. Khrushchev! Why are his speeches so moving? Because behind them is an enormous knowledge of life and the laws of its development, the most detailed acquaintance with practice, and a clear idea of the specific ways for their solution.[2]

A certain optimism began to creep back into Khrushchev's (and the regime's) statements during the summer of 1963. Perhaps on the basis of an overly confident assessment of his own political position, and in the glow of the successful test ban talks with the U.S. and U.K. in Moscow, Khrushchev for a time seemed more like the vigorous and commanding First Secretary of old. His speech in late July at a Hungarian-Soviet "friendship rally," for example, represented a forceful and fairly buoyant résumé of his views concerning peaceful coexistence toward the West, militant contempt toward the East (Communist China), strong anti-Stalinism, and economic emphasis on consumer welfare. His sole area of pessimism seemed to be associated not with the question of whether general war remained a real possibility (in this he was hopeful that indeed it did not), but rather with the problem of what the consequences of such a war would be. "To those [meaning those in Peking] who link the victory of socialism with [a world thermonuclear] war, we say that we can never agree to this. . . . No one knows in what plight the survivors would find themselves—even whether they would not then envy the dead!" [3]

Khrushchev's optimism, coupled with this horror of the consequences of war, was echoed later in the month by an unusually strong statement in *Pravda*. "Now nothing can stop the invincible movement of mankind toward communism started by the October Revolution," *Pravda* asserted, "except a world thermonuclear war." [4]

Though precisely how long this partial revival of Khrushchev's traditional optimism survived cannot be told, it is doubtful that it lasted beyond the late summer. By then the returns from the harvest should have been sufficiently alarming to have snuffed it out. And, indeed, there is little in Khrushchev's subsequent remarks, or those of his colleagues, which suggested that much hope had survived the summer. Later, the difficult decision to buy wheat from the West and the plenum on the chemical industry, which *inter alia* cut back Khrushchev's goal for fertilizer production, could not have done much to restore Khrushchev's confidence. And at the agricultural plenum in February 1964, Khrushchev, as indicated, apparently was forced to defend his program in the face of opposition from the military and other advocates of traditional investment patterns.

It was at about this time that official notice was taken of the rising tide of unhappiness and grumbling on the part of the people at large and of the efforts of anonymous figures allegedly seeking to capitalize on such discontent. "The year 1963 was an average one for the harvest," ran the story from "Radio Armenia," the apocryphal source of all such anecdotes, "worse than last year and better than next!"

A letter to *Izvestia* published on March 1, 1964, which was no doubt officially inspired, inveighed against all such forms of complaint. The writer professed disgust with those unpatriotic souls who spread tales about the bad harvest, food shortages, and the failures in the Virgin Lands. "All these 'fruits of wit' are nourished by somebody," he concluded, "and launched for a specific purpose. It seems to me that somebody needs to heighten an unhealthy interest in the extinguished political 'luminaries,' as certain persons describe the chief figures of the anti-party group." One of the implications of this was that it had occurred to some that the anti-party group, which had been publicly accused of opposing Khrushchev's Virgin Lands program, had been right after all. The public airing of such a sensitive issue suggested, in fact, that this opinion had become widespread and had become a cause for considerable high-level concern.

In late May, *Pravda* also hinted that all might not be well within the party. In a signed article dealing with the anniversary of the 13th Party Congress, the paper called attention to the evils of party disunity and the nefarious activities of those who sought to split the party apparatus away from the membership.[5] Such emphasis on the need for unity would have seemed gratuitous if all had, in fact, been well in the party of Khrushchev. Moreover, *Pravda*'s selective stress on certain of Lenin's policies seemed in fact to be merely a thinly disguised defense of Khrushchevian policies: emphasis on the need for material incentives for the peasantry, the need to strengthen the worker-peasant alliance (by, in effect, aiding the peasants), and the declamations against "any improvident haste, excessive regulation . . . which can often hold back the actual cooperation of the peasantry."

This *Pravda* article had been preceded by a campaign in the Soviet press against an alleged agricultural charlatan in Orenburg Oblast. Behind all the particulars and arcane rumblings—the volume and stridency of the campaign were grossly out of proportion with the importance of the alleged target—there was a strong suggestion of intense intra-party maneuvering at the very highest levels. Indeed, though the evidence is sparse and incomplete, it seems possible that the ultimate target of the instigators of the episode may have been Khrushchev himself.

On February 21, 1964, the journal *Selskaya Zhizn* (*Rural Life*) printed an article by one Sh. Khayrullin, the director of an Orenburg agricultural research institute, which, ac-

cording to later party commentary, was full of gross errors
and unscientific suppositions.[6] "The article is gaudy with
pompously illiterate expression, and confused, senseless conclusions," one subsequent, by no means atypical, comment
concluded.[7] Among other things, Khayrullin had sought to
establish for the whole of the Trans-Ural area a single sowing period, which, because of great variations in conditions,
was said to be absurd.

That the sins of this hitherto obscure agricultural specialist were not of solely academic interest was shortly thereafter confirmed when Khrushchev—very defensively, it
seemed—sought at the agricultural conference later in the
month to explain his own role in this embarrassing affair.
Khrushchev claimed that Khayrullin had approached him at
the February plenum and had "insisted" that an article he
had prepared be published. "In the presence of all the
plenum participants," Khrushchev said, invoking witnesses
to his innocence, "he gave me his article on the periods for
sowing and demanded that it be printed. I took the article
and asked the editorial board of *Selskaya Zhizn* to print it." [8]

That Khrushchev could not immediately recognize the
article for what it supposedly was—a dangerous piece of
nonsense—did not testify well to his qualifications as an agricultural expert, a status he had not been noticeably reticent
about in the past. That, in the face of Khayrullin's demands,
he, Khrushchev, had apparently felt compelled to succumb
meekly seemed somehow out of character for the otherwise
normally assertive First Secretary. And that he had raised
the subject at all, before a meeting of agricultural specialists,
after Khayrullin had been explicitly and forcefully repudiated in public media, seemed more than ordinarily suggestive of the probability that there was more going on here
than would meet the eye of the casual observer.

In late April, Khayrullin's boss, the secretary of the

Orenburg Oblast Agricultural Party Committee, was removed from his job in disgrace. V. A. Shurygin was accused of "not providing leadership" and of going along with the creation of a "Khayrullin myth." [9] The condemnation of the leadership of this key Virgin Lands province was unusually severe:

> From the moment of Khayrullin's appearance . . . in 1957, a special fame began to be created for him . . . [and] he was rapidly advanced in various organizations, and the obligatory application of his stereotyped recommendations was prescribed in the administrative procedures. Those who objected to Khayrullin were rebuked or even removed from their posts. . . . Even when Khayrullin's bankruptcy as a scientist was revealed, members of the Bureau . . . lacked the fortitude to oppose the pseudo-administrator of science.

Both Khayrullin, who apparently was, in fact, a charlatan (a poor man's Trofim Lysenko perhaps), and his superior, the ousted first secretary Shurygin, had long had close ties with CPSU Presidium member and agricultural specialist, Gennady Voronov. Voronov had brought Khayrullin into the oblast as his pet agronomist when Voronov had been first secretary of the Orenburg party committee.[10] Voronov's alleged agricultural know-how had been noticed, and praised, by none other than Khrushchev himself and Khrushchev had brought Voronov to Moscow and placed him on the Presidium.[11] Voronov's replacement in Orenburg was the same V. A. Shurygin, a longstanding protégé.

That Khayrullin and Shurygin were creatures of Voronov's, and that Voronov himself was a creature of Khrushchev's, was certainly no secret within the party. That a virulent and well-managed campaign against the former two also represented an attack on Voronov, and that this, in turn, touched on the First Secretary himself, was also no secret in the intricate world of Soviet politics. Only the previous summer, Khrushchev had personally seen to the appointment of Voronov to the chairmanship of a commission charged with recommending solutions to problems in the Virgin Lands.[12] And Khayrullin's heavily criticized article in late February had sounded suspiciously as if it might contain Voronov's recommendations.

The question remained, however, as to the episode's outcome. If Voronov now were removed, Khrushchev might be only one step away from an assault on his own preeminence. But, as it turned out, only the provincial figures were affected; Voronov was not. Either the plotters had been content with merely embarrassing Voronov, and through him Khrushchev, or they had somehow been blocked, perhaps by Khrushchev himself. But, even so, the affair as a whole probably indicated to the Soviet elite that all was not well at the top. As suggested earlier in *Izvestia*'s campaign against public grumbling, someone or some group had apparently sought to use the issue of faltering production in the Virgin Lands against the architect and principal enthusiast of the whole Virgin Lands campaign, Khrushchev, himself.

But Khrushchev turned seventy on April 17, 1964, and *Pravda* in its issues of April 17 through April 22 ran a total of eleven pages in praise of the First Secretary and in celebration of the event. Clearly, if embarrassed by the Voronov affair, Khrushchev and his colleagues were not going to allow it to interfere with outpourings of praise and reassurances to the party faithful that there was no cause for concern.

In July the Supreme Soviet was informed that Leonid Brezhnev had been released as Chairman of the Presidium of that body "in connection with the work occupying him in the Central Committee CPSU."[13] Khrushchev's old crony,

Anastas Mikoyan, was elected to replace Brezhnev.[14] At the time, the change seemed relatively ordinary. It was true that, as both a senior member of the Presidium and as a member of the Secretariat, Brezhnev had more than enough to do without also worrying about the demanding ceremonial duties of the Chairmanship of the Supreme Soviet (the titular presidency of the Soviet Union). And Mikoyan, as a venerable party leader and old Bolshevik, was an obvious candidate for the job.

The move, in fact, assumes political significance only in hindsight. Brezhnev's party status was, in effect, enhanced, as were his opportunities to improve his position vis-à-vis his competitor for the de facto post of heir apparent Nikolai Podgorny. Khrushchev, who probably was responsible for the change, may have wanted to make the balance of power between Brezhnev and Podgorny more nearly equal by allowing Brezhnev to spend more time on the important political work of the Secretariat. But if this is what Khrushchev intended, his scheme obviously worked too well. When Khrushchev was removed from office in October, Brezhnev was the man who stepped immediately into the First Secretaryship; it is likely that his ability to do so had been assured by the changes Khrushchev had arranged the previous July.

Domestically, the final two months or so of Khrushchev's reign were in some ways more active than the twelve which had immediately preceded them. Either because he had badly misjudged the tempo of the times and the strength of his opposition, or because, on the contrary, assessing these accurately, he had felt compelled to take the offensive, Khrushchev in the late summer of 1964 began to exhibit all the symptoms of a man preparing to introduce a radical new program and to purge those whom he feared would be inclined to resist. He was clearly impatient, and—apparently determined to give advance notice of this—he indicated in a number of public statements during July and August that he was tired of temporizing. The time had come for a major overhaul of national policy.

Just before leaving Moscow on an extensive tour of agricultural areas in the provinces, Khrushchev in late July called together a meeting of top cabinet officers and a number of economic and planning bosses.[15] As if to reassure himself that the ministers clearly understood him, he reviewed policy with these officials and discussed major "trends in elaborating the draft plan for the development of the national economy for 1966–1970." [16] Once more he placed principal emphasis on the chemical industry, intensified agriculture, and the raising of national living standards, *i.e.*, on the three keystones of the basic Khrushchevian program.

Next, once on tour, Khrushchev began to speak rather freely of what he had in mind for the next Central Committee plenum and to hint quite broadly of his desire for innovation. He complained about the existing system of supervision in the countryside and suggested in its stead something roughly akin to the U.S. county-agent arrangement, which he admired. In addition, he tentatively advocated a new way of organizing labor, assigning responsibilities, and providing for remuneration on the farm. He suggested that groups of peasants might be assigned specific tracts of land over which they would exercise full responsibility and from which they would be paid solely on the basis of the quantity and quality of their harvest. Finally, Khrushchev indicated that the entire Soviet system of agricultural management probably needed to be overhauled from the top down, suggesting the creation of a different administrative committee for each major crop.

The coming Central Committee plenum will discuss organizational questions of improving the leadership of specialized production. It has been suggested that we create union-republic administrations for grain, sugar beets, cotton, cattle, pigs, poultry, and other important agricultural products. . . . Under conditions of specialized production, a wide network of agricultural-industrial associations should [also] be created. Production, procurement, preservation, and initial processing of products are to be concentrated in the same hands.[17]

Khrushchev admitted to an audience in mid-August that "certain comrades" had complained about his revealing these proposals to the public even before the Central Committee plenum had an opportunity to discuss them. Obviously nettled, Khrushchev claimed that he was merely following the "Leninist style of work." Moreover:

Why should we make a secret of the fact that the Presidium . . . has decided to convene a plenary session and discuss a report on the deepening of production specialization, on the administration of specialized production? It is all the more irrational to make a secret of the proposals that will be discussed at the . . . plenum, of whose *vitality* I am becoming convinced as I acquaint myself with the experience of collective and state farms. We will lose much time if we do not speak of this now.[18]

This strong statement dealt with a matter which had in fact been of growing concern to party leaders and officials for some time, Khrushchev's propensity for appealing directly to the "people" over the heads of his colleagues. By so doing (principally through press accounts of his speeches), Khrushchev sought to give his proposals the cast of already adopted policies. This, in turn, was intended to intimidate skeptics or opponents by placing them in the position of resisting plans already advertised and touted by the party's top official—a position perilously close to the cardinal sin of "sowing the seeds of party disunity." In any case, Khrushchev's irregular procedure (which has been scrupulously avoided by the post-Khrushchev collective) could only create concern within the minds of the bypassed leaders that such high-handedness was likely to become the regular way of conducting business.

Pravda in mid-August created further anticipation of change with a major article dealing with the sensitive question of industrial management. The economist Vadim Trapeznikov, in a piece entitled, "For Flexible Economic Management of Enterprises," called for the expansion of the independence of individual manufacturing plants and firms and the adoption of a new system of profits as the "basic indicator" of performance in industry.[19] These notions, generally in the spirit of the "radical" proposals advanced the year before by the Kharkov economist Yevsey Liberman, were, unlike those of Liberman, treated not unsympathetically by the editors. *Pravda* issued a call for readers' comments, and such were soon forthcoming, almost all of them laudatory.[20]

In late September, Khrushchev decided to convene a meeting of top party and government personnel in order to issue a statement which, in effect, sought to proclaim the end of an era in Soviet economic affairs and the beginning of a new Khrushchevian epoch. The full text of his speech was never released, but even as later summarized, and perhaps toned down, in *Pravda* and *Izvestia*, Khrushchev pulled few punches.[21] The scene in the Kremlin thus must have been a dramatic one, even though few if any present were aware that this was to be the final statement of his career.

The chief task of this [forthcoming five-year plan] is a further rise in the living standard of the people. Whereas during the period of the first five-year plans and in the postwar years we laid chief stress on the development of heavy industry as the basis for an upsurge of the economy of the entire country, and on strengthening its defense capability, now, when we have a mighty industry, *when the defense of the country is at the proper level,* the Party is setting the task of the more rapid development of the branches that produce consumer goods. . . . Our country is now at the state of its development when *we should advance the satisfaction of the growing material and spiritual requirements of man into first place* in working out the long-range plan for the development of our economy. (Emphasis supplied.)

Khrushchev went on to outline his overall plans: the acceleration of agricultural production, much greater emphasis on the *quality* of goods (a scandalously neglected sphere of production), and the expanded output of consumer goods. The latter was to be achieved principally through growing stress on the appropriate raw materials base, more investment in the chemical, light, and food industries, and increasing emphasis on the role of heavy industry in such production. Khrushchev denied that such a program would endanger national security: "Of course, in doing so [raising living standards], we must always keep the country's defense at the proper level, because there may yet be adventures by the imperialist powers against the countries of the socialist commonwealth." [22]

This statement on military preparedness, almost an aside, reemphasized and in part repeated his earlier remark (above) to the effect that the nation's defense capacity had already reached this "proper level." It seemed clear from these two references that Khrushchev considered investment in the military establishment to be a subordinate proposition, one which—beyond a certain minimum—would be likely to receive only secondary consideration from the planners. Yet, Khrushchev contradicted this clear impression in another remark in the same speech: "The *further raising* of the country's defensive might in order to strengthen peace throughout the world is our constant concern." (Emphasis supplied.)

The implication of this last statement—ever-growing defense costs—is quite obviously different from that of the two preceding it—a freeze or even reduction of such costs. Khrushchev was perfectly capable of contradicting himself, but the bald nature of this particular conflict, together with the significance and delicacy of the subject, suggests deliberate obfuscation. It is tempting to speculate that the latter statement, a traditional formulation which was reassuring to the marshals and to conservative economic interests, was someone else's afterthought, added to the summary version of the speech.

Khrushchev's statements and activities during August and September, taken as a whole, must have strongly suggested to his colleagues and to the party apparatus that the First Secretary was about to give birth to yet another harebrained scheme. Though the precise form of his plans could only be guessed at, past performance would have suggested some sort of ill-considered and radical program designed to cure a large variety of ills with one massive and upsetting dose of medication. This, at any rate, seemed more and more often to be the essence of Khrushchev's style, and one can imagine the attitudes and fears of his subordinates as they awaited the revelation.

NOTES

1. *Izvestia,* July 10, 1963.
2. *Ibid.*
3. *Pravda,* July 20, 1963.
4. P. Pospelov in *Pravda,* July 30, 1963.
5. K. Kuznetsov and R. Terekhov, "Important Milestone in the Life of the Leninist Party," *Pravda,* May 26, 1964, p. 2.
6. See, for example, *Selskaya Zhizn,* February 25, February 27, and March 5, 1964. The issue of February 25 contained no less than three critical items on the subject.
7. *Ibid.,* February 25, 1964.
8. *Pravda,* March 7, 1964.
9. *Sovetskaya Rossiya,* April 29, 1964.
10. Voronov succeeded Polyansky as First Secretary in Orenburg in March 1957.
11. "The Building of Communism in the U.S.S.R. and the Development of Agriculture," Vol. I, p. 221, Dept. of Commerce, J.P.R.S.
12. See "On Several Questions of Raising the Economy of Lagging Kolkhozes and Sovkhozes": Note to the Presidium of the Central Committee, July 31, 1963, *Stroitelstvo Kommunizma* . . . , Vol. 8, pp. 62–87.
13. *Pravda,* July 16, 1964.
14. *Ibid.*
15. *Pravda,* July 25, 1964.
16. *Ibid.*
17. *Ekonomicheskaya Gazeta,* No. 40, 1964. For a further discussion of these proposals, see Harry Schwartz, *The Soviet Economy Since Stalin* (Philadelphia, 1965), pp. 174–175.
18. *Pravda,* August 10, 1964.

19. *Pravda,* August 17, 1964.
20. See, for example, *Pravda,* August 23, 1964.
21. *Pravda,* October 2, 1964; *Izvestia,* October 2, 1964.
22. *Ibid.*

7. Peace and Polemics

KHRUSHCHEV'S FOREIGN POLICIES during the last eighteen months or so of his reign were characterized in the East, toward Communist China, by invective and rapidly growing hostility; and in the West, especially toward the United States, by only very gradual and undramatic progress toward "peaceful coexistence." If, in domestic matters, Khrushchev encountered both frustration and failure, much the same could be said of his record in foreign affairs as well.

It was in the Soviet interest after Cuba, given the prevailing balance of power and Moscow's appreciation of the consequences of general nuclear war, to reach some sort of stable *modus vivendi* with the "imperialists," and the conflict with the Chinese surely encouraged the Soviets in their efforts to do so. As Moscow constantly asserted, a detente with the West did not imply the development of any genuine amity, and by no means would foreshadow an end to the U.S.S.R.'s active support of "progressive forces" in "wars of national liberation." But, overall, the U.S.S.R. was clearly anxious to avoid a confrontation with the West, and, with a few exceptions, avoided moves which would be likely to increase tensions. At the same time, it acted as if it fully anticipated a climax of some sort in its relations with China, and Khrushchev himself gave signs of actually looking forward to a final split in the movement. In neither area, however, did Khrushchev achieve his objectives: his efforts to come to a definitive break with the Chinese were abruptly thwarted by his removal from power, and his drive for detente was retarded both by the skepticism of opponents abroad and the opposition of skeptics at home.

The virulent attacks launched by Peking in the immediate wake of the Cuban crisis must have convinced Khrushchev that a showdown with China was inevitable.[1] His problem was no longer how to avoid such a confrontation but, rather, how to arrange it on the most favorable terms for the U.S.S.R. The nuclear test ban treaty of July 1963 was one crucial step in securing the Soviet Union's western flank, in order to turn eastward to deal with the Chinese. Moreover, the issue of nuclear testing in itself symbolized the root of the Sino-Soviet contest, and Chinese rejection of the treaty, which Moscow of course anticipated, provided the opportunity to shift the debate to the key questions of war and peace, on which the Chinese position was most vulnerable to Soviet attack. Since a majority of Communist parties, as well as underdeveloped countries, supported a relaxation of East-West tensions and some restraint on nuclear weaponry, the Soviets had in one move captured both the ideal issue and the best audience for the new debate with Mao.

The new phase of acute Sino-Soviet struggle began with the breakdown of the bilateral talks between the two parties held in Moscow from July 5 to July 20, 1963. Even before these negotiations had begun, however, a Chinese letter of

June 14 went beyond earlier polemics in revealing the breadth of the split which had evolved over the past three or four years; Peking left no area of Soviet activity, policy, or theory unscathed. The Chinese apparently were seeking in this approach to drag the Soviets through yet another debilitating exchange of shouts and insults. This tactic had hitherto worked to Chinese advantage because, as the challenger in the contest, Peking had almost always managed to gain from the Soviets' inability either to arrange an armistice or to fling back the Chinese gauntlet. At the same time, the Chinese were seeking converts throughout the communist world, and their open appeal to splinter groups and factions to preserve the movement's purity was a devastating tactic to counter, without forcing (and thereby accepting any blame for) a final, irrevocable break.

Each party had to maneuver carefully so that the onus for a split, when it finally came, would be placed squarely on the other side. But, as usual, the polemics gained a momentum of their own, and what began in June-July 1963 as a more or less theoretical discussion of the general line of world communism—the strategy of peaceful coexistence, and the nature of revisionism and dogmatism—quickly degenerated into simple name-calling and petty squabbling. This was especially true of the Soviets as Khrushchev's personal style of invective began more and more to show through in each successive diatribe.

The most interesting aspect of the initial phase of the new polemic was the revelation of how far the ideological quarrel had concealed the politics of power.[2] The Chinese divulged in an official government statement of August 15, 1963, that Khrushchev had concluded a treaty in 1957 promising to deliver to China a "sample" atomic bomb and to provide China with the technology to build its own nuclear weapons. This same statement also revealed that Khrushchev had repudiated this agreement on June 20, 1959.

On the Soviet side, concern over Chinese great power pretentions was reflected in the doctrine that (as spelled out in a government statement of August 21, 1963) Soviet nuclear power was sufficient for the entire communist world, and that any attempt to develop national nuclear capabilities was economically and militarily wasteful. Further, racism, which had long festered beneath the surface, now broke through, and the racial and national antagonisms between the two powers were revealed as deep and profound.[3] Finally, in September, the reliability of the Soviet commitment to defend China, embodied in Stalin's treaty with Mao in 1950, was also raised, and in the end it was apparent that neither side regarded the obligation as meaningful. In effect, Khrushchev marshaled all the conceivable arguments, both political and ideological, for breaking cleanly and finally with the Chinese.

A new high point, and a low point as well, was reached in September 1963. The Chinese began to publish a series of articles in *Red Flag* taking up in great detail all the issues they considered paramount in the dispute.[4] These articles continued at intervals until Khrushchev was overthrown and constituted a definitive statement of a Chinese position which has changed little since.

While the Chinese were trying to shift to the high ground of theoretical disputation, the Soviets were provoking and publicizing a sordid incident along the common border. Soviet authorities had detained the crew and passengers of a Chinese train and then had protested over the crude behavior of the detainees. Khrushchev's earthy delight in this affair can readily be imagined, as can the ability of the average Soviet citizen to recognize in it the very essence of *nekulturny*. According to the Soviet account:

Holding hands and having tied themselves to each other with belts, they [the Chinese] blocked entrances into offices, molested officers and other officials who walked past—grabbing their hands and feet and resorting to other hooligan methods, and flagrantly violating public order in the station premises. These unbridled rowdies went to such extreme cynicism that in front of the indignant passengers they provocatively violated elementary sanitary and hygienic norms in the station buildings.[5]

Polemics were not enough for Khrushchev, however. He needed a specific demonstration, before witnesses, that China was outside the pale, and for this he felt it necessary to convene another world conference of Communist parties. New pressures for such a conference first appeared in September, when the Soviets began to publish resolutions and statements of other parties favoring such a meeting.[6] But it soon became evident that Khrushchev had failed to gain enough support to convene such a conference. Indeed, several parties adopted a neutral position and expressed misgivings, and others, including the Italians, Rumanians, and Poles, were clearly upset by Khrushchev's scheme. The Italian party even published its reservations (and in October *Pravda* reprinted them).

In the face of this foreign opposition, and perhaps some domestic concern as well, Khrushchev took one step backward. On November 29, 1963 he dispatched a conciliatory letter to China calling for an end to polemics and mentioning the possibility of convening a new bilateral meeting. This move virtually acknowledged the failure of the initial phase of his campaign to muster support for the excommunication of China and undoubtedly represented a setback for the First Secretary. Any appeal to halt the polemics and return to the "normal" channels of interparty discussion was not likely to find much resonance among the Chinese, who had reason to feel relatively optimistic. Support for Peking was growing; the Soviets could cite the agreement of only about 60 out of the 90-odd Communist parties, and pro-Chinese splinter groups were sprouting almost daily. It was inevitable that the Chinese would press their advantage, and Khrushchev must have realized this.[7] Yet it was some months before he could resume the offensive against Mao.

There were several elements in the situation which must have given Khrushchev pause. First was the assassination of President Kennedy. This was a heavy blow for Khrushchev, not because of any special fondness he had for the President, but mainly because he had, in effect, surrendered a great deal of freedom of action to the U.S. His campaign against China depended to a great extent on demonstrating that the policy of peaceful coexistence was working and winning prestige and credit for the U.S.S.R. and this, of course, meant a continuing level of cooperation from Washington. But from July through November 1963, the only concrete advantage Khrushchev could show for his efforts was the purchase of large quantities of wheat from the U.S., and to some this smacked of begging from the imperialists. Moreover, the so-called detente had been marred by strange, seemingly inexplicable incidents, such as the abortive arrest in September 1963 of Yale University Professor Frederick Barghoorn (who was subsequently released after President Kennedy's personal intervention), and a highly flammable incident on the Berlin autobahn in October that threatened to explode the detente. Khrushchev was forced to retreat in both of these instances. And the Chinese had already pointed out that Khrushchev had "abandoned" the East Germans and was planning to sell them out entirely.[8]

As a result of all this, the detente was already brittle when the President was shot. The shock and uncertainty this event must have produced in Moscow may have caused Khrushchev to wonder whether the U.S. was in the grasp of an ultra-right-wing reaction. In any case, it was imperative for Khrushchev to confirm a continuing U.S. commitment to the detente, and the reliable Mikoyan was dispatched to Washington. Presumably, Khrushchev was satisfied with the assurances of the new President, who, in any event, asserted that he supported the policy of "discontinuing the cold war." [9] But Khrushchev's colleagues may have begun to question whether he was not predicating both his internal economic and military policies as well as his China policy on a dubious set of assumptions about the U.S. That deep concerns about the U.S. were indeed developing was later reflected in the famous memorandum by the Italian party leader, Palmiro Togliatti.[10]

If doubt had begun in this way to creep into the Presidium, Khrushchev's policy of forcing the issue with China no doubt fostered even more skepticism. Khrushchev regarded the split with China as irreparable and he had been proceeding in such a way as to hasten a final break. But in December 1963 (following Khrushchev's conciliatory letter to Peking), in a move perhaps reflecting the Presidium's fears and reluctance to sanction Khrushchev's apparent fatalism, *Pravda* specially admonished its readers:

> The open polemics have gone too far and in many instances have overstepped the norms of relations among fraternal parties. However, there is no need to dramatize the situation and to regard it as irreparable.[11]

For the remainder of the winter there was a stalemate of sorts, a pause in the most outrageous exchange of insults. Then, in February 1964, Khrushchev was able to break the Soviet reserve, but only after the Chinese, in a move he

probably anticipated, had launched (on February 4) another stinging attack on the Soviet party. This new Chinese
rebuff to the softer Soviet line preceded a Soviet Central
Committee plenum scheduled to consider agricultural policies; the business of the plenum was interrupted to allow Suslov to deliver a long, secret speech denouncing the Chinese
from every standpoint. Khrushchev had almost certainly intended to publish this new anti-Chinese platform immediately, but events suddenly took a complicated and unexpected turn: the Rumanians intervened with a plea for a
pause long enough to allow them to try one last effort at
mediation. The Rumanian leaders apparently felt that they
could use their increasingly independent line to persuade
the Chinese that they could win sympathy and support if
Mao would only meet the Russians halfway.

Khrushchev—lacking any convincing alternative—agreed
to hold up publication of the Suslov report. The Rumanians, led by Premier Ion Gheorghe Maurer, embarked on
a visit to China, North Vietnam, and North Korea; they
returned via Moscow in mid-March and met with Khrushchev. They reported the complete failure of their mission.
Khrushchev thus gained a free hand to resume the attack,
and on April 3 *Pravda* published the text of Suslov's indictment, together with an editorial explaining the recent events
and the new Soviet position. "Our further silence not only
would be of no benefit," *Pravda* declared, "but would contribute to the strivings of the Chinese leaders to disorganize
the ranks of the international communist movement. . . ." [12]

Khrushchev, however, did not have his own way entirely.
The Suslov speech, but not the Central Committee as a
whole, had endorsed the idea of another international conference. Indeed, the resolution of the Central Committee
called for continuing efforts toward "normalizing relations"
between the two parties.[13] Moreover, the stenographic text

of the plenum reveals that, of all the Presidium members, only the aged Otto Kuusinen spoke out in support of Suslov's statement.[14]

The Suslov indictment is also interesting on several other counts. It suggested that controversy within the Soviet party was welling up. Almost as an aside, for example, Suslov revealed that Molotov and some of the anti-party group had been expelled from the party, an issue which had long been debated and over which there had apparently been strong differences of opinion. In addition, Suslov vigorously defended Khrushchev personally; in retrospect he seems to have protested too much about the loyalty which Khrushchev commanded.

> In the struggle against the CPSU and its Leninist policy the Chinese leaders are concentrating their assault most of all on Nikita Sergeyevich Khrushchev who stands in the van of the wonderful processes that have sprung up in our Party and country after the Twentieth Congress and that ensure the successful progress of the Soviet people to communism. That is why they would like to isolate Comrade Khrushchev from the Central Committee for their subversive ends and to oppose our Central Committee to the Party and the Soviet people.[15]

This passage was followed by a fulsome tribute to Khrushchev's "inexhaustible energy," his "truly Bolshevik devotion," and his "sense of principle." Despite this and Suslov's claim that the party had never been so "united and monolithic," the astute observer might have recognized that implicit in the argument was the thought that Khrushchev was looming larger as the principal obstacle to a reasonable dialogue with China. And after Khrushchev's overthrow there were rumors that this report of Suslov's had indeed been the center of a controversy within the Presidium.

There is some evidence, in any case, that Khrushchev, obsessed with the Chinese issue, was riding roughshod over his more prudent colleagues. Thus, even before Suslov's report to the Central Committee, Khrushchev on February 12 had circulated a private letter to other parties (though not to the Chinese) criticizing Peking and indicating that at the forthcoming Soviet Central Committee meeting China would be condemned and a decision would be made on "collective measures" to reestablish unity (*i.e.*, a world conference).[16] When the Chinese learned of this new secret letter, they demanded an explanation, which they did not receive. Then, on February 29 the Chinese finally answered the original Soviet proposal for a world Communist meeting, actually agreeing to a conference, but seeking to defer it until after another round of Sino-Soviet talks in October. But the Soviets quickly replied to Peking and insisted on their own timetable: Sino-Soviet talks in May, a preparatory conference in June-July, and a world meeting in the fall of 1964.

The Chinese, of course, had no real intention of agreeing to a meeting, regardless of the timing. Peking too had apparently concluded that the break was inevitable and was hoping to maneuver Khrushchev into setting the final, fatal deadline. In May 1964, for example, the Chinese sarcastically proposed a series of preparatory meetings spreading over "four or five years or even longer."

Khrushchev finally lost patience with the dreary game and insisted on a specific date for the preparatory conference; the Soviet letter of June 15 was a virtual ultimatum, and, predictably, it drew a final Chinese rejection. "We will never take part in any international meeting or preparatory meeting which you call for the splitting of the Communist movement." Two days later, the Soviets issued invitations to the 26 members of the 1960 conference's preparatory editorial commission. The contents of these were not revealed, however, until August 10, in *Pravda*;[17] Khrushchev had crossed the Rubicon—the day for the final showdown was to be December 15.

It is quite likely that this last decision brought Khrushchev closer to his personal and political doom. The Chinese were not far wrong when they commented that "the day you call a schismatic meeting will be the day you step into the grave."[18] Figuratively speaking, at any rate, they were right. The meeting of December 15 was never held, and from the subsequent actions of the Brezhnev-Kosygin regime there can be little doubt that the scheduling of the meeting was regarded as a tactical blunder. After Khrushchev fell, one of the twenty-nine points of his indictment was that he had committed errors in his conduct of Chinese policy, leading the CPSU "almost to the opening of a dead-end street, involving the prestige of the CPSU in the preparation for a conference which finds not only the Chinese dissident, but also various Western Communist parties."[19]

Khrushchev's China policy might not have seemed so disastrous had he been able to substantiate his claim to a successful and productive Western policy. Yet he had only a modicum of success to show for more than a year of detente: a jointly sponsored UN resolution prohibiting the orbiting of nuclear weapons in outer space and an understanding with the U.S. to cut back on the output of fissionable materials. On the other hand, the original Soviet price tag for the test ban treaty had been a NATO-Warsaw Pact non-aggression treaty, and by late 1964 this issue was completely moribund. A primary dividend from the detente was also to have been a breakthrough in Western resistance to granting longer-term economic credits to the U.S.S.R. Indeed, much of Khrushchev's ambitious plan for the Soviet chemical industry had been founded on the assumption that imports of modern technology could be financed by new and lenient credits from the West. But this effort also had faltered.

One of Khrushchev's arguments for a relaxation of international tensions was that it would impose certain restraints on the U.S.; under such restraints the Soviets could continue to pursue vigorously their policies in underdeveloped areas against both Western and Chinese interests. Khrushchev had made some gains in this area, though it is doubtful that they had accrued from detente as such. His visit to the U.A.R. in May 1964, for example, was generally successful, though marred by some of his usual intemperate remarks. But in the same general area, he was mixing in a murky and potentially dangerous situation in Cyprus. In effect, Khrushchev had aligned the U.S.S.R. with the erratic Archbishop Makarios, thereby bringing on a crisis with Turkey. When the Turks bombed Cyprus in early August, Khrushchev resorted to a highly incendiary warning of retaliation. Moreover, he apparently promised to give Cyprus military aid.[20] He was ignoring the strong currents of *enosis* in Makarios' policy, and by playing the role of Cypriot protector he was, in effect, strengthening the chances that Cyprus would eventually come into the NATO sphere as part of Greece. Once he was overthrown, the new Soviet leaders quickly shifted to a more balanced line and implicitly criticized Khrushchev's Cyprus policy.[21]

Cyprus was not the only problem for Khrushchev in the late summer of 1964. There was Vietnam. Since the Laotian agreements of 1962, Khrushchev had slowly disengaged the U.S.S.R. from Southeast Asia. In 1963 after the signature of the test ban, the North Vietnamese party gradually moved into the Chinese camp, and Khrushchev made no effort to halt this drift. In fact, a Soviet note in late July 1964 seemed to forecast the U.S.S.R.'s political withdrawal from Indochina in the face of the worsening situation in Vietnam and

Laos.[22] It warned that the U.S.S.R. might have to give up its role as one of the cochairmen of the Geneva conference. When the U.S. bombed North Vietnamese naval installations in August after the Gulf of Tonkin incidents, Khrushchev made only a minimal response. The Soviet representative at the UN merely called for both sides to state their case in New York.[23] And for this neutral posture Khrushchev was resoundingly rebuffed by Hanoi and excoriated by the Chinese.

During roughly this same period, the Congo also had begun to boil over again. The Soviets, powerless to intervene effectively, were forced to issue the usual stale warnings. All in all, in light of the weak Soviet stand on Vietnam, it must have seemed that the detente was having a reverse effect: it was the "imperialists" who were exploiting the relaxation of tensions, not the Soviets.

Khrushchev continued to talk optimistically of detente, but by mid-September a new and harder line was beginning to emerge. Perhaps Khrushchev himself initiated the shift, but if so he was not its principal spokesman.[24] It was Mikoyan, for example, who stated on September 18:

> Unfortunately, there are still forces on our earth that guide themselves not by these bright beacons but by the flashes of explosion and the flames of fires. They are resorting to ventures in various parts of the globe, creating hotbeds of military conflict. One should openly state that the activity of the imperialists' forces in recent months has again led to the appearances of dangerous signs of aggravation of tensions in relations between states.[25]

But a far more extensive indictment of Khrushchev's generally optimistic view of the international situation was published in the Soviet Union shortly before these remarks of Mikoyan's—Palmiro Togliatti's "testament," which he wrote while vacationing in the U.S.S.R. before his sudden death. *Pravda's* publication of this astonishing critique was in itself an anomaly since it was larded with anti-Khrushchev positions. Of special interest concerning the international situation was Togliatti's deep gloom:

> We regard with a certain pessimism the perspectives of the present situation internationally and within our country. *The situation is worse than that facing us two or three years ago. Today there comes a more serious danger from the United States.* That country is passing through a profound social crisis. The racial conflict between white and colored people is only one aspect of this crisis. The assassination of Kennedy disclosed what point the attack of these groups could reach.
>
> One cannot under any circumstances exclude the possibility that the Presidential elections may be won by the Republican candidate (Goldwater), who includes war in his program and speaks like a Fascist. The worst is that the offensive he conducts moves increasingly to the right of the entire American political front, strengthens the tendency to seek in greater international aggressivity a way out of internal contradictions and to seek the basis for an agreement with the reactionary groups of Western Europe. *This makes the general situation somewhat dangerous.*
>
> Events in Vietnam, events in Cyprus, show how, above all, if the move to the right of the entire situation were to continue, we could suddenly be faced with very acute crises and dangers in which the entire communist movement and all the working class and socialist forces of Europe and the entire world would have to be involved. It is this situation, we believe, that one must take into account in all our conduct toward the Chinese Communists.[26] (Emphasis supplied.)

Togliatti's implicit indictment of Khrushchev's policy was, of course, a powerful blow to sustain, and, by early September, Khrushchev was in an increasingly ugly frame of mind. He had spent most of the summer touring in Scandinavia and then in Czechoslovakia. While in Prague he had reflected on the growing frustrations within the Communist world over China. The international conference, to which he was now committed, looked more costly each day. China and its allies, North Vietnam, North Korea, and Albania, would boycott the meeting; so would the Japanese, Australian, and New Zealand Communists. The Indian party was split, Castro was still on the fence, and the Italians would come to Moscow only to make trouble. Perhaps most important, within the U.S.S.R.'s own presumed sphere of influence, the Rumanians were, at best, doubtful starters.

Khrushchev discussed these frustrating difficulties in promoting his excommunication conference:

> The leaders of certain parties are taking a rather strange position in this question [of a conference]. . . . Certain leaders of fraternal parties, troubled by the situation that has arisen as a result of the activities of the Chinese leaders, are voicing doubts as to whether a conference . . . will do any good in the present conditions. . . . These comrades propose that the conference not be called just yet, but that preliminary work be carried out in an attempt to bring the viewpoints of all parties closer together. These are good desires, but how can they be implemented? [27]

Desperately trying to prove the validity of his case against China, Khrushchev unleashed a stream of invective, accusations, and petty insults. Typical of this desperate campaigning was *Pravda's* article in mid-September entitled

"Dope Merchants," which accused Peking of trafficking in human misery in order to finance its campaign against the U.S.S.R.:

> How is this muddy stream of lies and slander financed, how are the political rogues who perform according to Peking's cribsheets paid? . . . Largely with money received from the sale of dope. About $500 million annually falls into the hands of the present Chinese leaders from the contraband trade in narcotics. It has become one of the main sources of free foreign currency for the CPC leadership. The enormous sums obtained from it are spent on anti-Soviet propaganda and go to pay for the services of the puppets of the Peking splitters. . . . To adopt the methods of the imperialists, to come forth as partners of opium den owners is loathsome and monstrous, but it is logical for those who for the sake of their own hegemonic nationalist schemes disregard the vital interests of their own people, who try to poison the consciousness of their people with a potion even more venomous than opium.[28]

Also at work at this time was another issue, one difficult to assess, but one which may have played an even more direct role in Khrushchev's downfall. This was the question of Germany.

Khrushchev's global offensive against the West from 1957 through the Cuban crisis had rested heavily on a significant breakthrough in Central Europe. For Khrushchev, Berlin was the symbol. If the West could be forced to retreat on this highly charged issue, then Khrushchev could be assured that the Soviet empire in Eastern Europe could be consolidated. But this hope had, in effect, expired as the missiles were loaded onto the Soviet ships in Havana harbor for return to the U.S.S.R. For five years Khrushchev had been on the offensive, but now, in 1963 and 1964, he had been thrown back on the defensive. New pressures on Berlin were not only as risky as ever, and probably much more so, but Cuba had proved beyond question that the U.S. was prepared for the most serious and dangerous confrontation. It was up to Khrushchev therefore to devise a new line on Germany.

After the Cuban crisis the U.S.S.R. had, in effect, called off its campaign against the Allied presence in West Berlin, had signaled its readiness to postpone the related question of a German peace treaty indefinitely, and had already gone a long way toward solving the question of East German viability with the erection of the Berlin Wall in 1961. Washington had been induced to work for detente; London had been enthusiastic about the prospects; Paris, to the extent that it remained skeptical, was not a major problem. But Bonn apparently remained unmoved and (in Soviet eyes) an active proponent of traditional cold war politics vis-à-vis the Soviet Union. None of the U.S.S.R.'s moves toward Germany and Berlin, and none of its moves toward detente, had had any noticeable relaxing effect on the West Germans, who were more inclined to read American appeasement than Soviet concessions into any improvement in Soviet-U.S. relations.

Not much happened, however, until the spring of 1964. But then German Chancellor Ludwig Erhard, in the confusing atmosphere of East-West detente, launched a trial balloon—it might be worthwhile, he suggested, to meet with Khrushchev. Moscow showed considerable interest. A trip to Bonn might just be the dramatic event that Khrushchev could exploit, not only to demonstrate the validity of his Western policy, but to compensate for the coming blowup with China. Obviously, if Khrushchev could prove not only that the threat from the West was under control but that detente had even opened up the long-awaited cracks in the West German scene, then he would appear more than justified in cutting completely the Eastern tie to Peking.

But before Khrushchev could contemplate a move in West Germany he had to make sure of his connection to East Berlin, and there had recently been signs of coolness in his relations with Ulbricht. The East Germans were unhappy with the detente and the new nationalism flourishing in Eastern Europe. Afraid to confront Khrushchev directly, they nonetheless lashed out at the hapless Czechs for encouraging the "Trojan Horse" of West Germany in Eastern Europe. Actually, Bonn's new eastern policy had made some gains, especially in establishing trade ties with Rumania, Poland, and Bulgaria. In the process of the negotiations, these countries had acknowledged a semi-legal relationship between West Berlin and Bonn, a highly alarming precedent for Ulbricht to contemplate. The East Germans were thus frustrated, worried, and perhaps alarmed by Moscow's inability or unwillingness to take a hand.[29]

Khrushchev's reaction was to invite Ulbricht to Moscow and on June 12, 1964, to sign a new treaty of mutual assistance and friendship. The East Germans were presumably placated by this new official reassurance. But then a strange interlude occurred. The treaty should have been ratified immediately. The East German *Volkskammer* was convened in July, but, incredibly, the treaty was not even on its agenda. The Soviets also made no move toward ratification. Instead, July saw Khrushchev's son-in-law, Adzhubei, depart for a tour of West Germany. It was apparent that this was no mere journalistic survey, that it was, in fact, a high-level political fishing expedition. Adzhubei was duly received by high political personages, including Erhard, and apparently solicited an official invitation for his father-in-law to visit Bonn. And, almost as if to add to the bizarre atmosphere, he dropped tantalizing tidbits here and there which seemed anti-Ulbricht in intent. He is said, for example, to have written Ulbricht off as a cancer victim with only a short time to live.[30]

Upon his return to Moscow, Adzhubei launched a series of articles in *Izvestia*. Though not of great interest, there were hints in these of the preparation of a new and softer Soviet political line toward Bonn. Adzhubei's general conclusion was, for example, that Bonn stood at a crossroads, and, while refusing to predict new directions, he claimed, "Among people of various political, social and economic positions in the Federal Republic of Germany, there is maturing, or beginning to mature, a more reasonable perception of the contemporary world, from which there is no escape." [31]

That Adzhubei's mission and meddling into such crucial affairs as German policy caused resentment and concern was evident in the anti-Khrushchev documents circulated after his fall. Specifically, Khrushchev was charged with nepotism and with "initiatives taken without consulting the plenum (sic) of the Central Committee, like that of entrusting Adzhubei, who was invited to Western Germany by a group of six German newspapers, with a special diplomatic mission. . . ." [32]

Signs of tension over Khrushchev's German policy persisted, and the ever-perceptive Chinese, sensing trouble in Soviet-East German relations, thrust a stiletto into Ulbricht's back. On September 8, *People's Daily* claimed that the Soviet Union had made the German Democratic Republic an "object of barter," and by various quotations created the impression that there was "discord" in relations between East Berlin and Moscow. This was indeed embarrassing, and the East Germans rebutted the Chinese on September 20 in *Neues Deutschland*. Nevertheless, tensions remained. Contrary to advance rumor, Khrushchev did not choose to

visit East Berlin for the celebrations of East Germany's fifteenth anniversary. Instead, Brezhnev was announced as the
delegate. Then the East German deputy premier, Willi
Stoph, suddenly arrived in Moscow on October 1, but only
after Khrushchev had departed on vacation. Stoph, whose
purposes were never revealed, returned to Berlin within a
few days, apparently in order to attend an East German
party Central Committee meeting.

Soviet reassurances to the East Germans were eventually
forthcoming, but they were not from Khrushchev. Instead,
in early October, Brezhnev, Kosygin, and Suslov all made
speeches endorsing an orthodox hard line on Germany.[33] The
treatment of Suslov's statement was particularly interesting
in that *Pravda* deliberately edited out references to Khrushchev in his remarks about Soviet-East German solidarity.[34]
Perhaps the enigmatic Suslov was well aware that such references would soon be going out of style.

It may be that Khrushchev actually had no grandiose or
specific plans to alter the U.S.S.R.'s German policy. Indeed,
it is difficult to see how he could. But surely there was nerv-
ousness over his intentions.[35] In any event, once Khrushchev
had been removed, all talk of a high-level visit to Bonn, or of
significantly improving relations with the Federal Republic,
was thrust aside.

Despite all of these oddities, difficulties, and problems
that crept into Soviet foreign policy during 1964, it is
difficult to conclude that Khrushchev's foreign policy was a
primary cause of his undoing. His successors have changed
tactics and altered priorities, but there has been as yet no
profound revolution in Soviet diplomacy. But Khrushchev's
highly personalized style of conducting foreign policy, together with his notable lack of important achievements after
the nuclear test ban, must have contributed to the
underlying malaise in he Kremlin. None of his colleagues

could predict with much confidence the consequences of his policy, particularly in regard to the showdown with China. But it was apparent to them that his policies were proving increasingly costly, and they must have wondered more and more whether he was worth the price.

NOTES

1. See Richard Lowenthal, "The Prospects for Pluralistic Communism," *Dissent*, Winter 1965, pp. 103 ff.; also Lowenthal, "Russia, China and the West: A New Balance," *Encounter*, October 1963.

2. For a review of Soviet and Chinese polemics and maneuvering, see William E. Griffith, "Sino-Soviet Relations, 1964–65," *China Quarterly*, January-March 1966, No. 25, pp. 3–143.

3. K. Nepomnyashiy, "Whose 'Theory' Is This?" *Pravda*, August 27, 1963.

4. The series of Chinese letters began on September 6, with a *Red Flag–Peoples Daily* article: "The Origin and Development of the Differences Between the Leadership of the CPSU and Ourselves."

5. TASS, September 9, 1963.

6. See Harry Gelman, "The Conflict: A Survey," *Problems of Communism*, Vol. XIII, March–April 1964.

7. *Ibid.* Also Wolfgang Leonhard, "A World in Disarray," and Kevin Devlin, "Boring from Within," *ibid.*

8. NCNA, August 23, 1963, *Peoples Daily* article, "To What Position Has the GDR Been Relegated?"

9. *Pravda*, December 31, 1963.

10. See also *Pravda*, "The Hopes and Anxieties of Americans," December 25, 1963.

11. *Pravda*, December 6, 1963.

12. The complete text of the Suslov report was published in English by Crosscurrents Press, in the series *Soviet Documents*, Vol. II, No. 16, April 20, 1964.

13. *Pravda*, April 3, 1964.

14. *Plenum Ts K KPSS, 10–15 Febralya 1964g. Stenograficheskaya Otchyot*, pp. 559–610.

15. *Soviet Documents*, Suslov Report.

16. For the various Soviet and Chinese letters see Current Digest of the Soviet Press, Vol. XVI, No. 30, August 19, 1964.

17. CDSP, August 26, 1964, Vol. XVI, No. 31; *Pravda*, August 10, 1964.

18. NCNA, August 30, 1964.

19. *Paese Sera* (Rome), October 30, 1964, pp. 1, 12.

20. For Soviet commentary on the Cyprus situation see *Mizan Newsletter*, Vol. 6, No. 8, September 1964.

21. Podgorny's speech in *Pravda*, February 7, 1965.

22. *Pravda*, July 27, 1964.

23. *Pravda*, August 8, 1964.

24. See Khrushchev's interview with *Pravda* and *Izvestia* on August 6,1964, and his speech to the Moscow Military Academy, *Pravda*, July 9, 1964.

25. *Soviet Documents*, October 19, 1964.

26. *The New York Times*, September 5, 1964.

27. CDSP, Vol. XVI, No. 36, September 30, 1964, p. 7.

28. *Pravda*, September 13, 1964.

29. *Der Spiegel*, August 19, 1964, p. 18.

30. *Ibid.* August 5, 1964, p. 20.

31. CDSP Vol. XVI, No. 33, p. 24.

32. *Paese Sera* (Rome), October 30, 1964.

33. Speeches by Kosygin, *Pravda*, October 4, 1964; Suslov, *Pravda*, October 6, 1964; Brezhnev *Pravda*, October 7, 1964.

34. *Pravda*, October 6, 1964.

35. *The New York Times*, November 16, 1964.

8. The Fall

When it finally came, the fall from power of Nikita Sergeyevich Khrushchev was sudden, swift, and complete. No confessions were forced from his lips by Stalinist jailers, as had happened with Zinoviev and Kamenev and countless others, and there was no period in which he was forced to tarry at the summit in a kind of Khrushchevian cat-and-mouse game, as had happened to Voroshilov and to Bulganin. But there was, nonetheless, very little mercy in the way that his comrades disposed of him. Indeed, they almost threw him away, as if by the scruff of the neck. His collapsed form was shaken out over an alley behind the Central Committee building and then tossed onto the general refuse heap of Soviet political life.

Khrushchev's fall from power was a surprise—to him, to his people, to the world at large, indeed to everyone except the members of the party cabal which plotted and carried out his overthrow. Though some effort was made to put the proceedings into a legal context—votes were taken in the Central Committee and in the Presidium of the Supreme Soviet—the real move against Khrushchev came as the consequence of conspiracy and stealth, not votes. Given

Khrushchev, the resourceful fighter, and the Soviet constitutional system, which is silent on the ways of retirement and succession at the very top, there could have been no other way. The coup probably would not have succeeded, or at least would have been accomplished only with great pain and disarray, if it had not come as a total surprise to its principal victim. As it was, Khrushchev did not learn of his dismissal until he had hurriedly returned to Moscow from the Black Sea coast and found that all the reins of power had been taken from him during his absence.

There were few if any real signs during August and September that Khrushchev was in any sort of especially serious political difficulties. In hindsight, however, it is possible to discern not only the broad harbingers of the October events but also a specific development which, deliberately or not, conveyed some sense of impending upheaval: the appearance of the memorandum by the Italian Communist Party leader, Palmiro Togliatti, in which the Italian leader revealed a deep weariness and expressed (though not by name) his profound discontent with Khrushchev's larger failures. It is now clear that Togliatti's mood was not that simply of a discouraged outsider, but was, in fact, symptomatic of the views of an ever-widening circle of Khrushchev's intimates in Moscow.

Togliatti's testament refused to sanction Khrushchev's drive for an international Communist conference to read the Chinese party out of the movement.[1] Moreover, Togliatti, in a tone of pessimism typical of his entire paper, looked with dismay at a number of developments within the U.S.S.R. and suggested the need for fundamental changes in Soviet attitudes. Concerning one of Khrushchev's principal policies and self-styled achievements, de-Stalinization, Togliatti was acutely unhappy.

The [Soviet] criticism of Stalin—there is no need to hide this—has left rather deep traces. The most serious thing is a certain degree of skepticism with which also some of those close to us greet reports of new economic and political successes. Beyond this must be considered as unresolved the problem of the origin of the cult of Stalin and how this became possible. To explain this solely through Stalin's serious personal defects is not completely acceptable.[2]

Togliatti also suggested that, in addition to its failure to come to grips with the genesis of Stalinism, the Soviet leadership apparently could not be trusted to be of one mind concerning the issues of the day. In a passage which clearly implied that all was not well with Khrushchev's leadership of the Soviet party, Togliatti confessed confusion and recommended a startling remedy.

Some situations appear hard to understand. In many cases one has the impression there are differences of opinion among the leading groups, but one does not understand if this is really so and what the differences are. Perhaps it could be useful in some cases for the socialist countries also to conduct open debates on current problems, the leaders also taking part. Certainly this would contribute to the authority and prestige of the socialist regime itself.[3]

Togliatti's strong unhappiness with Khrushchev was soon, of course, to be vindicated by the Soviet leader's summary removal from office. And Togliatti's charges were soon, of course, to be echoed and amplified throughout the Soviet press. But Togliatti was not destined to live to see either day. And there were to be no "open debates of current problems" before Khrushchev was forced from power—unless

Togliatti's lone effort be counted as such—and none afterward. Instead, there was to be a series of strange incidents involving that least open of all Soviet political institutions, the KGB, the Soviet secret police.

Though still enormously important and, especially in times of domestic stress, a vital element of the Soviet political structure, the Committee of State Security (KGB), was not the power and feared instrument under Khrushchev that it had been in Stalin's time. Placed under the control of the party after Beria's removal in 1953, so that it could not again be used to terrorize the party, it acted independently or as the tool of factional interests only in rare instances. One or two of those rare instances may have occurred in the fall of 1964.

A highly exotic incident involving the KGB occurred in September, and it created a flurry within the diplomatic community in Moscow and threatened for a time to disrupt Soviet-West German relations. A minor West German diplomat, who was said to have had esoteric intelligence functions, was physically attacked in bizarre fashion while he was visiting an historic church on the outskirts of Moscow. The man was gravely injured, apparently by mustard gas sprayed on his leg. Somehow he survived, returned to embassy sanctuary in Moscow, and eventually was flown out of the country and hospitalized in West Germany.[4] The KGB apparently had engineered the entire affair, hoping at a minimum to rid itself of a dangerous adversary, and at a maximum to embarrass official relations between Moscow and Bonn at a time when Khrushchev was preparing for a visit to West Germany.

The KGB seemed unusually active throughout September. Early in the month, *Pravda* and *Izvestia* both featured a number of articles on the late Soviet master spy, Richard

Sorge, who, in keeping with international tradition, had hitherto received no official recognition whatsoever. Together with some earlier favorable and fulsome press references to the secret police for their "humane" treatment of some of Stalin's victims during the purge years, this sudden publicity for Sorge as a Soviet hero suggested an attempt to glorify the KGB, though to what particular purpose (other than to appease any secret police appetites for public acclaim) could not then be seen.

Later in the month, the United States military attache in Moscow, an assistant U.S. military attache, and a British military colleague were the victims of an unprecedented KGB raid on their hotel room during a stopover in their trip across eastern Siberia. In gross, blatant, and cynical violation of their diplomatic immunity, a KGB team forcibly held and searched the attaches. The Soviet foreign office subsequently protested to the United States and Great Britain, claiming that the attaches had violated international law and practice by carrying out "inadmissible activities" and espionage.[5] The two Western governments, of course, rejected the notes and countered with vigorous protests of their own.

Mysterious incidents such as these suggested a growing deference to the power and influence of the KGB, and, as such, were ominous. They did not appear at all consonant with Khrushchev's policies, and, indeed, it is certainly conceivable that this flexing of muscles by the police was somehow related to the forthcoming move against the First Secretary.

Khrushchev left Moscow on September 30 for another sojourn at his villa on the Pitsunda peninsula near Sochi. His leavetaking was abrupt and, in retrospect, somewhat strange. He was, after all, still entertaining a distinguished foreign guest, Indonesian President Sukarno, and by leaving

Moscow on September 30 he missed Sukarno's farewell soiree and departure ceremonies on the following day. Moreover, another important visitor, Willi Stoph, the new premier of East Germany, was due to arrive in Moscow on October 1. Especially in view of all that had occurred concerning the German question in the previous weeks, Khrushchev would normally have been expected to stay in town to see Stoph. On the other hand, perhaps Khrushchev felt that it would simply be too painful to explain his contemplated visit to Bonn to yet another East German functionary.

The circumstances of Khrushchev's hurried exit from Moscow gave rise to rumors that he had in fact been sent away by the Presidium.[6] No doubt his colleagues preferred that Khrushchev allow them some respite to ponder his sweeping new plans for the economy. But it is hardly believable that anyone could have "ordered" Khrushchev to leave town. Moreover, Khrushchev was too experienced in the intrigues of Kremlin politics to leave town if he suspected that real trouble was brewing; it was during his brief visit to Finland in 1957 that Malenkov and Molotov had sprung the plot that nearly succeeded in bringing him down.

In any case, Khrushchev by no means rushed off to seek seclusion. He stopped first at Simpferopol in the Crimea and conferred there with Petr Shelest, the first secretary of the powerful Ukrainian party, and Ivan Lutak, the party secretary of the Crimean province. Accompanying Khrushchev was his agricultural advisor, Vasily I. Polyakov, a former party journalist who had been elevated to the Secretariat by Khrushchev, and whose task during the vacation in Sochi probably was to prepare the detailed text of Khrushchev's report to the party Central Committee meeting scheduled for November, even though the Presidium had not yet approved it.[7] (Soon after his mentor was overthrown, Polyakov too was relieved of his offices.)

When Khrushchev reached his retreat at Sochi he did not spend all his time in contemplation of the wonders surrounding him—three villas, heated swimming pools, indoor badminton courts, and secret blue telephones amidst the dark green pine forests.[8] On the contrary, he received a steady stream of visitors: a parliamentary delegation from Japan, a similar group from Pakistan, the leader of West Germany's illegal Communist Party, Max Reiman, and the last foreigner to speak with Khrushchev while he was still in power, Gaston Palewsky, a French cabinet minister. All this hardly suggests the activities of a man kept under wraps by the Presidium.

Khrushchev, playing the role of head of state in Sochi, obviously failed to realize how deep the disillusionment of his colleagues back in Moscow had become. The economic reorganizations and priorities which he had proposed in September were fast becoming the last straws. The crisis with China, together with the complications it was causing in Eastern Europe, was sufficiently alarming in itself. But added to it were hazardous ventures in the West, beginning with the proposed trip to Bonn. And the way Khrushchev had decided to bring all of these matters to a head within a single brief period, and in rapid sequence—first a Central Committee meeting on the economic reforms; next, in December, a showdown with Peking; and finally, probably early in the new year, the journey to West Germany—was simply too much.

It was too much for the Presidium and, in fact, too much for Khrushchev, because he had committed a fatal error: he had provided the basis for an overwhelming coalition against him. In the past, he had manipulated the balance of forces in the Presidium, playing one against another, shifting his own position first to one side and then the other. In 1953, he had joined Stalin's heir presumptive Malenkov against the sinister Beria, then in 1957 had used the military against Malenkov, and finally, later in the same year, had moved against the military (Marshal Zhukov). All this he had done in the name of the party. But as time went by it became increasingly apparent that he was unwilling—as perhaps Brezhnev now is not—simply to serve as an agent of the party. He felt compelled to shape it, to redirect it, and to bend it not only to his will but also to his new way. The most alarming symptom of this had been his party bifurcation scheme of 1962, and it is small wonder that many in the party—whose cause had been discovered by Kozlov—had fought back and not forgiven.

Now, in the fall of 1964, he had offended nearly everyone, not just the party apparatchiki: the military, already under strong pressure for budgetary restraint and fearing more; the heavy industrialists, natural allies of the military and in the first lines of those who bore the brunt of Khrushchev's scorn and erraticism; the state bureaucrats, harried, hounded, and bewildered, subject to one reorganization after another and fearful for their prerogatives and their very jobs; and even the intellectuals, whose hopeful vision of Khrushchev as a reluctant patron of the freedom of the arts had been so jarred by his intemperate and Philistine behavior of late 1962 and early 1963.

Moreover, this wide-ranging discontent had communicated itself to, and was reflected in, the very top bodies of both party and state. Dissension was prompted there, in addition, by high-level policy concerns, such as Khrushchev's handling of the German, Chinese, and Vietnamese questions, his concepts of military strategy, even his boorish conduct abroad. And dissension was also provoked by high-level political ambitions; it was easy after his ouster to see that at least three of Khrushchev's successors—Brezhnev, Suslov, and Kosygin—enjoyed immediate and meaningful gains in power.

Brezhnev

If there was, then, this coalition of discontent, it was informal, inchoate, and in search of a leader. Brezhnev, sensing this, was in a good position, indeed, the *best* position, to transform unhappiness and frustration into political action and to capitalize on Khrushchev's apparently growing weaknesses. Brezhnev's prime rival and opponent under Khrushchev had been Kozlov. With Kozlov struck from the lists, ailing and discredited, only Podgorny could challenge Brezhnev as the senior party figure, *i.e.*, as the new "second secretary." There is some reason to think that Khrushchev, especially after the unpleasant incident with Kozlov, had intended Brezhnev and Podgorny to be contending heirs apparent. But, if so, he should have known that the contest was unequal. Brezhnev simply held too many advantages.

Indeed, Brezhnev's credentials for the First Secretaryship of the CPSU of the 1960s could not have been better selected by computer. He was a son of the proletariat, a Russian from the Ukraine, a graduate metallurgical engineer, a wartime general officer (political), and a party professional (first secretary of oblasts and republics) par excellence.[9] He rose high under Stalin—candidate membership on Stalin's large Presidium of 1952—but not too high. He attached himself to Khrushchev's rising star early on and served him long and well, but not too well. And, during all this, he apparently knew how to avoid a reputation for excessive attachment to any particular person or cause. Neither fanatic nor liberal, he was a good and safe party man and a practical politician. If few were inspired by him, fewer still were alienated.

Suslov

The ideological malcontent, Mikhail Andreevich Suslov, a member of the Central Committee since 1941 and a leading regime figure since 1947, had been profoundly disturbed by Khrushchev's failures in the international movement and, at the same time, had looked for a revival of doctrinal orthodoxy on the home front.[10] In Brezhnev he could see a man more susceptible to his influence than Khrushchev, more sympathetic to traditionalist views and less so to those of the new party technocrats.

By himself, Suslov was of limited consequence. He exercised strong influence, though not power, only over party conservatives; he had not built up a large personal following within the central party apparat in Moscow and had had no opportunity to do so in the provinces. But Suslov no doubt found kindred souls among the military-heavy industry clique and he was not without respect at the top levels of the party itself.

Brezhnev, of course, was an opportunist and would not have been inclined to jeopardize his position in the hierarchy by moving against Khrushchev on the mere say-so of a Suslov and some aging marshals. And, indeed, though the self-interest of many of the marshals may have inclined them toward the views of Suslov, the military as a whole were far from united.[11] Their titular spokesman, the Minister of Defense, Marshal Rodion Malinovsky, had been handpicked by Khrushchev in 1957 when Malinovsky had willingly served as the hatchet man in the dismissal of Marshal Zhukov. Serving under Malinovsky were a conglomeration of military groupings roughly divided between Marshal Sergei Biryuzov's "rocketeers"—much favored by Khrushchev—and the old ground force heroes of World War II who felt that Khrushchev's budgetary ax was aimed at their heads, or at least at their beloved tanks and artillery pieces.

Kosygin

It was among the more pragmatic elements that Khrushchev had found his most useful allies in his long campaigns against the conservatives. The chief pragmatist spokesman in the Kremlin was generally believed to be Alexei Kosygin, the young mayor of Leningrad before the war, who had risen to a first deputy premiership and membership on the party Presidium.[12] Kosygin was no champion of pop art, Western jazz, or mod clothes, but he *was* an able advocate of economic and administrative rationalization and sought to bring about a better balance between the demands of the heavy industry-military establishment and the needs of the consumer. In this sense, Kosygin could be counted on to lend a strong voice in support of the goals of many of Khrushchev's economic schemes. But Koysgin was also an engineer, a technocrat, and a realist. He appreciated scientific solutions; he sought orderly planning; and he worked for clearly defined channels of authority. Although he had, of course, compromised his principles many times, economic plans had been his life's work, first under Stalin and then under Khrushchev.

In the spring of 1963, Kosygin had worked with his fellow Leningrader, Kozlov, to restructure the administration of the Soviet economy under a Supreme Economic Council. If he was at that time in sympathy with some of Khrushchev's concepts—especially his efforts to achieve greater balance between the various claimants for investment funds —he nonetheless could not have approved of Khrushchev's bifurcated party reorganization, his blindly impulsive methods, and his wildly enthusiastic, almost fanatic devotion to particular schemes and pet industries, such as chemicals. The situation was not totally different in the fall of 1964. While Kosygin could accept and even support greater emphasis on the lighter industries, or a greater injection of "Libermanism," this was to be accomplished, in Khrushchev's "harebrained" plan, by creating administrative chaos: specialized production committees for each major crop and seventeen new regional administrations. Also, despite Khrushchev's brave words about his new economic goals, the hardheaded Kosygin must have realized that Khrushchev was still seeking panaceas and trying to accomplish everything on the cheap. Kosygin and his economic planners could not simply return to the drawing boards, as ordered, and prepare a truly feasible "long-term" plan.

With Brezhnev increasingly ambitious, Suslov ever more discontented, and Kosygin in a state of mounting frustration, the foundations of a tentative alliance had been laid. Together, these three men—the party bureaucrat and politician, the party ideologue and propagandist, and the government chieftain and economic planner—represented broad and diverse interests within the elite, and at least two of them, Brezhnev and Kosygin, probably could command the loyalty and support of a considerable body of officials at many levels of the establishment.

It is doubtful, however, that these three or any other group began hatching a plot the moment Khrushchev boarded the train for the south. No doubt all three had thought how simple life would be if they were in charge, rather than the irascible and quixotic First Secretary. But planning against him was exceedingly dangerous business. No such secret could be kept for long. A quick and decisive blow, à la the abortive attempt of Molotov-Malenkov and company of 1957, might work, provided, of course, that the mistakes of that hapless group could be avoided.

There were many practical problems involved in staging a coup against the First Secretary. For one, Brezhnev was scheduled to begin a visit to East Germany on October 5 to help celebrate the fifteenth anniversary of the founding of the German Democratic Republic. Normally, Khrushchev would have attended—he had gone to Czechoslovakia for a much less auspicious anniversary in August—but he apparently preferred not to make any speeches in East Berlin which could cast a shadow over his planned foray into West Germany. Accordingly, it was announced on September 28 that the Soviet delegation would be led by Brezhnev and would include the first secretary from Belorussia, Kiril Mazurov. A week later the group left Moscow for Berlin. Brezhnev was obviously not then in a good position to move against Nikita Sergeyevich. And he obviously was not the kind of man who would set things in motion only then to leave town, trusting his own fate to the hands of other conspirators. Indeed, it is likely that little if anything was done to prepare for an anti-Khrushchev coup while Brezhnev was still in East Berlin.

During the interval from Khrushchev's departure from Moscow on September 30 until Brezhnev's return on the evening of October 11, political life proceeded normally in the capital, at least on the surface. The top leaders were active in public, receiving the new East German premier and attending the opening of an East German exhibit honoring the fifteenth anniversary. Most of the Presidium was in town. Notable absentees in the first days of October were Andrei Kirilenko, Brezhnev's old protégé from Ukrainian days, who was apparently on vacation, and Anastas Mikoyan, who had joined Khrushchev on the Black Sea by October 3.

Mikoyan and Khrushchev had vacationed together before. It is only in hindsight that anything unusual has been read into Mikoyan's presence in Sochi in October 1964. It has been suggested, for example, that Mikoyan went to Khrushchev to warn him of impending troubles, or that, conversely, Mikoyan acted the role of front man for the plotters, preventing Khrushchev from suspecting that ominous events were in train.[13]

A simpler explanation is likely. Mikoyan had no foreknowledge of a plot because at that time (on October 3–4) there was no concrete plot. He did not return to Moscow to convey Khrushchev's ultimatum to the Presidium to approve the new economic plans (as has also been suggested), but remained in Sochi until at least the afternoon of October 12, when he and Khrushchev appeared together on television, chatting with the three new cosmonauts as they orbited in the Voskhod. Had he known of or suspected the impending upheaval, it is highly doubtful that Mikoyan, an astute practitioner of the art of survival, would have been content to rest in Sochi or to allow himself to be so closely identified with the doomed Khrushchev.

The first days of October slipped by without unusual incident. The summary of Khrushchev's important speech on the economy to the Presidium and Council of Ministers— made sometime in late September—appeared in the Moscow papers on October 2 and created some interest in the West and presumably at home as well. The next day Khrushchev's absence from Moscow was confirmed in the Soviet press by a short account of his stopover in Simpferopol, where he had visited a state farm and dropped a few remarks about better crops.

On October 3, safely at rest on the Black Sea, Khrushchev met with the Japanese delegation. One of the members of this delegation later said that, while he was talking to

Khrushchev, Mikoyan entered the room unexpectedly and sat down to listen. This seemed strange to the visitor. Khrushchev talked of world events and emphasized that he expected both Japan and West Germany to play an important role in UN affairs, an odd remark since Germany was not a member of the UN.[14] On the following day, the Pakistani were received and Khrushchev and Mikoyan posed for a group picture.

On October 5, in Moscow, Brezhnev went to the airport and boarded the plane for Berlin; waving goodby were Presidium members Kosygin, Podgorny, and Voronov and party secretary Vitaliy Titov. By late afternoon Brezhnev was in the embrace of Walter Ulbricht, while his comrades in Moscow were turned out for a gala at the Kremlin to pay homage to East Germany's fifteen years of survival. Only Kosygin appears to have begged off and missed the festivities. About this time, Marshal Malinovsky also left town, traveling to Czechoslovakia, where he remained until he returned to Moscow on the evening of October 9.

It is possible (though unlikely) that the plot was conceived and put into motion during these days by the principals who remained in Moscow—Kosygin and Suslov. But, if so, they acted more or less under the eye of Khrushchev's loyal lieutenant, Nikolai Podgorny, one of the more mysterious actors in the October crisis. Podgorny had no particular reason, either ideological or personal, to oppose Khrushchev, who had plucked him out of the Ukraine and made him at least an equal contender for the position of heir apparent. And Podgorny's activities in the last few days before the crisis suggest that he was unaware of what was soon to take place. Podgorny traveled to Kishinev on October 9 to represent the central leadership at the anniversary celebration of the Moldavian Republic. While there he made a long speech which, in almost every detail, supported Khrushchev. He even interjected a personal note, mentioning that he had spoken with Khrushchev (in Sochi) on the telephone just before leaving Moscow and that he brought Khrushchev's personal greetings to Kishinev. This was faithfully reproduced in *Pravda* on October 11.

Some of the other leaders, of course, were doing the same sort of thing, *i.e.*, praising Khrushchev, but they did so without this personal note. In any case, if Podgorny had in fact conversed with Khrushchev by telephone, and if Podgorny had smelled a conspiracy at the time, he probably would have found some way to alert his boss. But Khrushchev, in Sochi, showed no signs of having received any warning of what was in store for him. If, on the other hand, Podgorny knew of a plot and was covering up, his subsequent behavior and the fate of his protégés in the post-Khrushchev period indicate that he was ill-rewarded for his duplicity.[15] The hard fact is that Podgorny could have had no rational motive for joining a plot which would replace Khrushchev with Podgorny's arch rival, Brezhnev.

Podgorny remained in Moldavia through the weekend, listening to praise of "our dear Nikita Sergeyevich" from the unsuspecting Ivan Bodyul, the party first secretary of Moldavia. When Podgorny finally departed for Moscow on Sunday, the other leaders were beginning to reassemble for Monday morning's business, a meeting of the Presidium to "endorse" Polyakov's draft for the Central Committee of Khrushchev's new economic program.

This meeting of the Presidium must have been very much on Brezhnev's mind when his flight touched down at Vnukovo airport on the afternoon of October 11. He knew that the leaders might not be of a mind to submit meekly to Khrushchev's dictates and that debate over Khrushchev's radical proposals might be long and stormy and lead to a full-blown crisis in the leadership. He also knew that not much time remained to plan strategy or to prepare a move against Khrushchev, if it should come to that. President Dorticos of Cuba would arrive in Moscow on Wednesday, October 14, and he would expect to see Khrushchev soon thereafter. The timing of Khrushchev's return to Moscow also would be guided by the success of the space venture which was already nearing blast-off. If the flight of the three-man Voskhod was successful, then Khrushchev would surely return to Moscow to lead the welcoming festivities.[16]

Brezhnev was met at the airport by Suslov and the two men undoubtedly conferred that evening. Brezhnev must have confirmed Suslov's view that Khrushchev's handling of the German question was creating immense problems. Brezhnev must have had his ears filled in East Berlin with the complaints of the East Germans over Khrushchev's forthcoming visit to Bonn. Speculation of a "sellout" was spreading throughout the European press, and even the Chinese were gleefully and openly fishing in these troubled waters. Brezhnev for his part had revealed his (and his hosts') sensitivities by making a strong defense of the East German position in his major speech in Berlin:

> Only shortsighted politicians who are completely divorced from life, such as certain gentlemen on the banks of the Rhine, can console themselves with the hope of making some kind of decision or deal behind the back of the GDR (German Democratic Republic) to the detriment of its national interests and security. No, my worthies, this will not happen. You can never expect this *from us.*[17]

Brezhnev and Suslov may have made the final decision to try to remove Khrushchev as they conferred on that evening of October 11. In reviewing the strengths and weaknesses of their position, the two men may have counted noses and decided that in any such effort they could rely on the votes of five full Presidium members out of a total of ten (excluding the ailing and inactive Kozlov). Suslov might have told Brezhnev that, in general, sentiment against Khrushchev had not abated during Brezhnev's absence. He might have added, in particular, that Kosygin was in no mood to accept Khrushchev's policy proposals without putting up a stiff fight, and that Dimitry Polyansky—the Presidium member most closely associated with rural affairs—was dismayed by Khrushchev's arbitrary formulation of agricultural policy and furious at Khrushchev's capricious favoring of the hack agriculturalist Polyakov. For his part, Brezhnev could surely have pledged the vote of his old protégé from Dnepropetrovsk, Andrei Kirilenko.

Brezhnev and Kosygin knew, of course, who was likely to be found on the other side. Khrushchev, Mikoyan, and Podgorny could be expected, initially at least, to form a solid triumvirate. And these three could probably depend on the support of the aging Nikolai Shvernik and of Gennady Voronov, a Khrushchevite who had long vied with Brezhnev's man, Kirilenko, for position and power within the Russian Republic.

A clean five-to-five split on the Presidium would simply not be sufficient for the plans of the conspirators. An old fighter like Khrushchev would try to manipulate the members of the Central Committee in his favor, especially if the word was out that the anti-Khrushchev group lacked a majority on the Presidium. A plenum of the Central Committee, which Khrushchev could call, might thus lead to a vote against the plotters and to disaster; this is precisely what had happened in 1957 to the Molotov–Malenkov group even though it had first succeeded in mustering a majority on the Presidium.

The anti-Khrushchevites therefore had first to find some

way of isolating Khrushchev from his principal supporters or, failing that, isolating the Khrushchev-Mikoyan-Podgorny triumvirate from the levers of power. And this, obviously, had to be done before the Central Committee had had an opportunity to render its verdict. In effect, matters had to be arranged so that the Central Committee would be persuaded either that the coup against Khrushchev was accomplished fact or that it could be prevented only through means no longer at the Committee's disposal.

Two organizations would ultimately hold the key to success or failure, the military and the secret police. Approaching either was bound to be risky. A premature leak to Khrushchev could be fatal, and Khrushchev had, of course, made sure that the secret police and the top military command were heavily weighted with handpicked appointees. Nevertheless, both the army and the police had reason to be restive under Khrushchev, and the conspirators could always try to suborn key individuals by promising them expanded power and prestige or—especially in the case of the military —greater solicitude for the needs of their particular institutions.

An approach must have been made to Alexander Shelepin, who, though not formally in charge, still exercised considerable influence over the secret police through his close friend and colleague, KGB chief Vladimir Semichastny. If Shelepin were won over, the secret police could probably at least be neutralized. Shelepin's rise and subsequent fall after Khrushchev's overthrow indicates that he was not only persuaded where his future lay, but apparently (and mistakenly) saw the opportunity to take the grand prize in the process.[18]

Brezhnev also had a separate channel into the police-intelligence combine which must have served him well. One of his closest associates from the old days in the Ukraine,

Nikolai Mironov, was the chief of the party organs section of the Central Committee.[19] This section had its fingers in a wide variety of activities and, in effect, was the party's channel for controlling police and intelligence work. The threat of Mironov might have played a role in influencing Shelepin to cast his lot with the conspiracy. (Oddly enough, Mironov died in a plane crash in Yugoslavia shortly after the coup had succeeded; he and the rocketeer, Marshal Biryuzov, who also perished, had been sent to Belgrade to explain events to President Tito.)

The army apparently did not join the conspiracy wholeheartedly. The evidence of divisions and doubts in the military came to light during the last days of the plot. *Red Star* on October 14 published an article by Marshal Biryuzov, the Chief of Staff, praising Khrushchev.[20] The appearance of this piece at this late date—*i.e.*, well after the Presidium had decided to move against Khrushchev—suggested that Biryuzov was making a gesture of defiance or, at the very least, had been deliberately kept in ignorance of the decision. Another senior officer, Marshal Pavel Rotmistrov, speaking on the same date, listed Brezhnev among the heroes of the Ukrainian war effort but placed him below his usual position in the pecking order.[21] Another gesture of defiance? Certain other military figures, including the political commissar, Alexei Yepishev, continued to praise Khrushchev in public articles well after such praise was politically imprudent. Apparently he too was at least ignorant of the events which had taken place in the Kremlin.[22]

But it was the Minister of Defense, Marshal Malinovsky, who held the key. Even if the military were divided, his joining the anti-Khrushchev group would be a powerful sign of the strength and breadth of the First Secretary's opposition. And, by virtue of his high office, Malinovsky could probably control physical security in and around Moscow and, if need be, perform the role Zhukov did for Khrushchev in 1957, insuring that transportation into the city was available only for the right people.

Though Malinovsky had served Khrushchev well, he had increasingly in recent times indicated displeasure over the drift of Khrushchev's military policies, especially his predilections for downgrading the ground forces.[23] As one of the World War II commanders of the vast tank armies that broke through the German lines into Central Europe, it was difficult for old soldier Malinovsky to adjust to Khrushchev's radical notions about modern war. It was this growing disenchantment that made Malinovsky vulnerable to an approach from the dissenting politicians. That they succeeded later became dramatically evident when Malinovsky—speaking during the confrontation between Khrushchev and the Central Committee—declared the support of the Soviet armed forces for the opposition.[24]

At 10:47 on Monday morning, October 12, the Soviets launched a space ship with three cosmonauts aboard. On the third orbit, Moscow radio and television began to carry a conversation between the cosmonauts and Khrushchev. Mikoyan was at Khrushchev's side, and, as Khrushchev put it, was "literally grabbing" for the telephone. After the usual congratulatory pleasantries, Khrushchev told the senior cosmonaut, Colonel Vladimir Komarov, that he would be greeted in Moscow with great celebrations. The conversation ended, but was rebroadcast throughout the rest of the day and was dutifully reprinted in the Soviet press on Tuesday.[25] This event, of course, meant that Khrushchev was still in touch with Moscow and apparently had no hint of the crisis. It also put the plotters on notice that the First Secretary would soon leave his hideaway on the Black Sea and return to the capital. Time thus was running out.

Sometime during this last week, perhaps on Sunday or Monday, Khrushchev made a blunder which must have played into the hands of his opponents. He ordered the Foreign Ministry to send "regrets" to Bonn over the mustard gas attack on the West German official in early September, thus completely reversing the previous Soviet refusal to apologize for the incident. This high-handed action—taken solely to smooth the way for his controversial trip to West Germany —must have embarrassed Foreign Minister Gromyko, infuriated the KGB, and provided more ammunition for the Brezhnev coalition. Indeed, perhaps it was this last bit of maneuvering by Khrushchev which brought the full support of the KGB behind the conspiracy.[26]

The Presidium hastily assembled on Monday afternoon. Eight members were present at the outset and Mikoyan may have joined the session later. The hard-core of anti-Khrushchevites—Brezhnev, Kosygin, Suslov, Polyansky and Kirilenko—probably pressed for Khrushchev's immediate and summary removal. Brezhnev no doubt announced that his moves had the approval of both the KGB and the military, with the personal endorsements of Shelepin, Vladimir Semichastny and Marshal Malinovsky. But Podgorny, who now learned of the magnitude of the plot for the first time, was probably highly reluctant. He may have been joined by Shvernik and, later, by Mikoyan. Voronov was probably shrewd enough to recognize that the tide was running against the First Secretary and may thus have kept silent or sided with Brezhnev.

This lack of unanimity in the Presidium may have led to a face-saving compromise for the recalcitrants: Khrushchev would be offered the opportunity to resign gracefully, with honor, from his high party and state posts and with continued membership on the Central Committee. But if, as all suspected, Khrushchev refused to resign, then the issue would be placed before the Central Committee with the Presidium's recommendation that Khrushchev be voted out of office. In either case, honorable retirement or purge, the Central Committee had to be summoned as soon as possible to give its formal approval. Such a compromise would, of course, have been tantamount to a victory for the Brezhnev forces.[27]

Orders were duly sent out to members of the Central Committee to assemble in Moscow by Wednesday at the latest.[28] Brezhnev, now probably in good control of the party machinery, no doubt got the word around to selected members that Khrushchev's fate already had been decided. What happened next is, unfortunately, still veiled in mystery. Some observers believe that the Presidium gave orders for the cosmonauts to de-orbit well ahead of schedule, to insure Khrushchev's immediate return to Moscow.[29] This cannot be proven, of course, and it seems a dubious proposition. It is true, however, that the Voskhod landed in Kazhakstan (not the normal landing zone) on Tuesday morning, October 13, despite a plea from Komarov to be allowed to remain in space another twenty-four hours.

Another version of events is that on Monday evening or Tuesday morning an emissary from the new collective leadership in Moscow was dispatched to Sochi to see Khrushchev. The emissary is said to have been D.F. Ustinov, the civilian czar of Soviet defense industries, a first deputy premier and, though not a Presidium member, a major figure in the hierarchy. Ustinov was a Leningrader and something of a management specialist who presumably had links to Kosygin. He was also a representative of the military-heavy industrial clique and the chairman of the Supreme Economic Council which had been established in the spring of 1963, during the period of Khrushchev's decline, but which had been largely ignored by Khrushchev ever since. Ustinov almost certainly had little regard for Khrushchev, and there were many signs that the sentiment was reciprocated. In any case, Ustinov is supposed to have informed Khrushchev that the Presidium had encountered problems with his new economic program, and that, as a consequence, his presence was required in Moscow.[30]

Whether, in fact, Ustinov carried out such a mission for the Presidium cannot be confirmed. But it is true that by Tuesday Khrushchev apparently suspected that something out of the ordinary was going on in the Kremlin. Perhaps his suspicions had been aroused by some minor irregularity in, for example, his communications with Moscow. Or perhaps he had received some sort of warning from his son-in-law, Adzhubei, who, as a member of inner party circles and as editor of *Izvestia,* might have picked up reports of an unusual Presidium meeting. Or, finally, perhaps he had heard something from Mikoyan, who may have returned to Moscow on Monday in time to attend the actual meeting. (Mikoyan's retirement from the Presidency in 1965, might have been forced, in part because he had acted essentially in Khrushchev's interests or, alternatively, had sought to play a double game.)

In any case, on Tuesday morning, October 13, Khrushchev abruptly changed his schedule for the day. He had intended to have a leisurely lunch with his guest, Gaston Palewsky, the French cabinet minister who had arrived in Sochi after seeing Kosygin in Moscow. But Palewsky was told at 7 in the morning that plans had changed: Khrushchev could not lunch with him but would receive him at 9:30. The meeting took place on time, and the Frenchman found Khrushchev in an amiable, if slightly nervous, mood. Khrushchev remarked, perhaps presciently, that "a political leader should never leave power of his own free will."[31]

After about half an hour, an aide said the meeting would have to end, claiming that Khrushchev's presence in Moscow was required by the cosmonauts (who themselves did not arrive in Moscow until Saturday).

Palewsky was ushered out, and Khrushchev followed soon thereafter. By early afternoon his plane had landed in Moscow. The last battle had begun.

Khrushchev left the plane and, according to some accounts, was met by both Semichastny and Shelepin.[32] The former, acting as KGB chief, is said to have placed Khrushchev in "protective custody". Semichastny may indeed have met him, and Khrushchev would surely have seen the significance of Semichastny's presence. It is doubtful, however, that any form of even de facto arrest was involved or intended. The new collective leadership would hardly have wanted to start matters off with such a heavy-handed display of Stalinist tactics. Two or three of the Presidium members were still probably unhappy with the majority action and had probably been promised that Khrushchev would be allowed to retire in dignity. Further, the Central Committee had as yet to sanction the moves of the Presidium, and even the figurative manacling of the First Secretary could only have helped his cause.

In any event, Khrushchev, presumably accompanied by at least Semichastny, proceeded directly to the Kremlin to confront the Presidium. There he found Brezhnev in the chair, a circumstance which forced Khrushchev to seat himself in an unaccustomed place at the side of the table. Khrushchev, almost certainly puzzled and belligerent, may have begun by demanding an explanation of what was going on. Brezhnev would have answered for the group. At some point, Khrushchev evidently protested that the Presidium lacked competence to vote on his retirement and may also have claimed that it did not have the right to assemble without his concurrence.[33] Brezhnev would have brushed such protests aside.

Once it had become clear that Khrushchev had no intention of "retiring," Suslov apparently took the floor to present the Presidium's case against the style and substance of Khrushchev's conduct of national affairs. The Suslovian brief covered now-familiar ground: Khrushchev's arbitrariness and high-handed methods, his efforts to build a personality cult, his errors of policy dealing with China, his handling of the Cuban missile crisis, and so on. Khrushchev evidently made no real effort to defend himself against these charges for it was already clear that he could not sway the majority ranged against him. He did, however, fall back on the tactic that had saved him in the confrontation with Molotov and Malenkov in 1957—he demanded an immediate Central Committee meeting. This, of course, had been anticipated, and Khrushchev was informed that the Central Committee already had been summoned. At this point, if not sooner, he must have begun to suspect that the die was cast.[34]

The Central Committee meeting probably began early on Wednesday, October 14. It was a long gruelling session. Suslov spoke at great length, and, *inter alia*, presented in detail the bill of particulars which later were circulated to the party faithful as the "twenty-nine points." [35]

Suslov's speech may never be published. Its essence, however, may actually have been previewed in an extraordinary article published in a Soviet journal in August, *i.e.*, well *before* Khrushchev's fall.[36] The article, appearing in *Problems of History, CPSU*, contained praise of Khrushchev and his policies but, in its particulars, actually seems to be directed against him. It asserted, for example, that "certainly the masses have the right to control the leaders, to check and replace them if they do not cope with matters or if they carry out an incorrect line." Elsewhere, the article warned: "If the leader ceases to carry out the will of the party and begins to set himself against the masses, and does not listen to its voices, his one-man management loses its reasonable basis and sooner or later he will suffer failure. . . ." One can well imagine Suslov using these very words to justify the actions of the Presidium.

One can also imagine Suslov's holding forth in a general way about the sins of Khrushchev in a manner quite similar to the article's discussion of the various errors a Soviet leadership—presumably any leadership—can fall into.

Economism

Khrushchev had often (and understandably) been accused of emphasizing economics to a fault and to the exclusion of other important areas of emphasis, such as ideology. In the Communist lexicon, and, specifically, in Chinese charges against Khrushchev, the term "economism" was reguarly used to describe such a deviation. The tendency is mentioned in the article and vigorously condemned.

> We recall the "economists" with their orientation toward spontaneity to the detriment of the organization of professional revolutionaries. . . . Lenin scornfully rejected these demagogic attempts to set the crowd against the "bosses," to inflame bad and vain instincts in the former, and to sap the unity and stability of the movement by disrupting the confidence of the masses in the dozen smart men.

Demagoguery

Khrushchev sought to improve the quality of the party apparatus and considered this a key part of his overall program. In addition, Khrushchev often tried, especially when campaigning for innovations, to avoid regular channels and to appeal over the heads of the apparatus to other agencies and to the people. Thus, to the discomfiture of the party regulars, he liked to convene greatly expanded Central Committee plenums and conferences, to which were invited all manner of functionaries and experts not in the apparatus. Khrushchev had, in addition, long argued for a shake-up of party officials (the "cadres"), had demanded that older leaders make way for younger ones, and had carried out a long campaign against the old Bolsheviks in the anti-party group. The article seemingly takes disapproving note of all these tendencies.

> During the Soviet period, Trotsky resorted to . . . demagogic methods. Disguising himself with revolutionary phrases, he slandered the party apparatus and the old Bolshevik guard, [and] demanded a "shake-up" of the leading cadres. . . . Lenin considered the demagogues the worst enemies of the working class.

Commandism

Khrushchev, as was so emphatically stated following his ouster, had a penchant for reorganizations and sweeping decrees. He sought panaceas and tried to impose his magic solutions uniformly, without adequate regard for local conditions, as, for example, in his 1961 campaign to plow up and plant crops on grasslands. Moreover, Khrushchev, as previously indicated, may have been the indirect target of the Orenburg Oblast purge (the Voronov affair) in the spring of 1964. The article ties these two matters together.

> Excessive administrative rule engenders rule by command, and it leads directly to making bureaucratic decrees and to replacing a creative, flexible leadership

with stereotyped directives and petty supervision by officials. Precisely this occurred, for example, in Orenburgskaya Oblast [where] former [party] leaders . . . imposed uniform, stereotyped directives and plans . . . and smothered the creative initiative of the [farmers, local officials, and experts]. . . . [The imposition of uniform agricultural rules] without regard to conditions, and crude suppression of protests against this, inflicted heavy damage on the economy. As a result . . . the authority of some "infallible" leaders burst like a soap bubble.

Promisism

Partly because of the extraordinary publicity given them, and partly because of their extravagant nature, Khrushchev's promises to the Soviet people to raise their living standards dramatically, and especially his promises to surpass even the United States in the production of meat, milk, and butter, were among the best-known statements ever uttered by the First Secretary. Surely many in the party viewed these promises as cheap tricks, as demagogic efforts to woo the masses. In any case, Khrushchev clearly was in this sense the most "promising" of all Soviet leaders. The article takes note of "promism" and then, significantly, calls attention to the necessary restraining power of the collective.

> But the authority which is built on playing with the masses, on indulging backward attitudes, and on giving out unfulfillable promises is also cheap. A leader must always be principled, correct, and honest with the people. The Leninist rule is not to flatter the masses, not to play with them, and also not to lose touch with them. . . . *This means always to rely on the collective, believe in its powers,* and not to swim with the current, adapt to the moment, and be a demagogue. (Emphasis supplied.)

Conceit

Khrushchev's fondness for himself and for his own proposals was not an easy matter to conceal, and, indeed, Khrushchev did not normally seek to do so. He was also inclined, on this account, to surround himself with a personal staff of flatterers (*e.g.*, Adzhubei) and yes-men (*e.g.*, the various ministers of agriculture). But, according to the article in question, such propensities are entirely unworthy of the leader.

> Some leaders try to create their own authority on the basis of servility and toadyism. These are rotten supports. . . . Authority can grow and become strong only on a healthy, genuinely Bolshevik basis. . . . M.I. Kalinin warned that the party leader must in no case become proud and conceited.

Khrushchev was forced to sit on a side bench in the Central Committee meeting hall throughout the Suslovian *tour d'horizon*, listening, no doubt in anguish, to condemnations along the lines suggested above. Witnesses have reported that he was red-faced and highly agitated. But there is no detailed account of the rebuttal he was allowed to deliver after Suslov sat down, merely a very general description of its content as aggressive, insulting, and profane.[37] He is said to have been interrupted several times from the floor, but he rambled at length. At last he sat down, exhausted and apparently resigned. Dimitry Polyansky followed him, charging Khrushchev with manifold errors specifically in the area of agricultural policy.

Finally, the question of Khrushchev's removal from all his party posts was put to a vote. Khrushchev lost, decisively, but the issue was by no means decided unanimously —Khrushchev may have received up to one-third of the total.[38] Khrushchev then submitted a written resignation but plaintively appealed to the members of the Central Committee to recommend that he be given the position of Minister of Agriculture in the government. Many of them laughed.

Khrushchev's last statements to the Central Committee have, of course, never been officially revealed. Oddly, even poignantly, his final published words were thus those initially spoken over Soviet television to the trio of cosmonauts circling the earth on October 11. *"Do svidania,"* he had said. "Good-bye."

NOTES

1. *Pravda,* September 10, 1964; translated in *The New York Times,* September 5, 1964.

2. *Ibid.*

3. *Ibid.*

4. *The New York Times,* October 14, 1964.

5. *Pravda,* October 7, 1964.

6. Details of the last few days before Khrushchev's fall can be found in a wide variety of sources. Two full-length accounts are Martin Page, *Unpersoned* (London, 1966), pp. 65–100; Michel Tatu, *Le Pouvier en U.R.S.S.* (Paris, 1966), pp. 433–460. Shorter accounts are Henry Tanner, *The New York Times,* October 22, 1964; Stephen Rosenfeld, *Washington Post,* October 22, 1964; Harrison E. Salisbury, *The New York Times,* October 17, 1964; Harry Schwartz, *The New York Times,* November 1, 1964; Michel Tatu, *France Observateur,* October 22, 1964; K. S. Karol, *Le Monde,* October 23, 1964.

7. Preparing memoranda for Presidium approval prior to a Central Committee meeting was typical of Khrushchev's style. See Jerry F. Hough, "Enter N.S. Khrushchev," *Problems of Communism,* July-August, 1964.

8. For a firsthand description of Khrushchev's Black Sea retreat see *Time,* August 16, 1963.

9. For a biography of Brezhnev, see George W. Simmonds (ed.), *Soviet Leaders* (New York, 1967), pp. 21–29. See also Linden, *Khrushchev and the Soviet Leadership,* biographies at annex, pp. 231–246.

10. See Simmonds, pp. 108–115.

11. The best accounts of the conflict between Khrushchev and the military are Matthew P. Gallagher, "Military Manpower: A Case Study," and Thomas Wolfe, "Political Primacy vs. Professional Elan," both in *Problems of Communism,* May-June 1964.

Also Victor Zorza, "Khrushchev's Losing Fight with the Marshals," *Life*, November 6, 1964, and Thomas Wolfe, *Soviet Strategy at the Crossroads* (Cambridge, 1963).

12. See Simmonds, pp. 40–50.

13. Page, pp. 67, 76, and Tatu, pp. 434–435. The latter mistakenly claims that Mikoyan departed from Sochi on October 4 because he was not listed with Khrushchev as receiving the Pakistani. In fact, he and Khrushchev posed for a picture with the Pakistani that was published in the English-language *Moscow News*.

14. Warren Unna, *Washington Post*, October 23, 1964, quoting Ahchiro Fujiyama.

15. Podgorny's protégé Vitaly Titov, for example, was removed from the Secretariat after Khrushchev's fall, while Vladimir Shcherbitsky, Brezhnev's colleague, made an immediate comeback in Podgorny's bailiwick, the Ukrainian party.

16. Western reporters already were speculating on a feat in outer space; *The New York Times*, October 12, 1964, U.P.I. from Moscow.

17. *Pravda*, October 7, 1964; C.D.S.P. Vol. XVI, No. 40, p. 9.

18. Simmonds, pp. 87–95.

19. Mironov's career and the details of his connections to the defense industry are indicated by his obituary in *Pravda*, October 22, 1964.

20. *Red Star* (*Krasnaya Zvezda*), October 14, 1964.

21. *Pravda Ukrainy*, October 15, 1964.

22. *Komsomolskaya Pravda*, October 14, 1964.

23. See the articles by Gallagher and Wolfe in *Problems of Communism*, May–June, 1964.

24. United Press International, Moscow, October 29, 1964, quotes "Communist sources" for Malinovsky's role against Khrushchev.

25. *Pravda*, October 13, 1964.

26. *The New York Times*, October 14, 1964.

27. Rosenfeld, *Washington Post*, October 22, 1964, claims that the Presidium was split 7–2; he quotes "diplomatic sources."

Tanner, *The New York Times*, October 22, 1964, asserts that Podgorny and Mikoyan were reluctant to endorse a coup, and that Mikoyan was faced with a virtual "ultimatum" when he returned to Moscow on Monday evening.

28. Tanner, *The New York Times*, dates orders for the Central Committee from late Monday.

29. Page, pp. 77–78; *The New York Times*, October 14, 1964.

30. *Time*, October 30, 1964. A slightly different version of the Presidium's insistence on Khrushchev's return is quoted from the *Daily Worker* by Schwartz, *The New York Times*, November 1, 1964.

31. *Newsweek*, October 26, 1964.

32. Page, p. 84; Tatu, p. 448; no other accounts mention Semichastny's presence at the airport to meet Khrushchev.

33. The statutes of the Soviet party contained no provisions regulating Presidium meetings. The 1957 crisis between Khrushchev and Molotov-Malenkov provided some precedents; in that instance Molotov convened the Presidium. See Roger Pethybridge, *A Key to Soviet Politics* (London, 1962), pp. 93 ff.

34. In 1957, Khrushchev challenged the right of the Presidium to dismiss the First Secretary and succeeded in forcing a meeting of the Central Committee even though he was outvoted 7–3, with Suslov neutral. The contrast was obvious in 1964 when the majority convened the Central Committee.

35. The twenty-nine points, attributed to Suslov, were published by *Paese Sera*, October 30, 1964.

36. I.A. Alexsandrov and P.I. Kotel'nikov, *Voprosy Istori KPSS*, No. 8, 1964, pp. 29–43.

37. All accounts agree that Khrushchev's defense was vitriolic: Rosenfeld, *Washington Post*, describes it as including "profane and personal accusations." Tanner, *The New York Times*, states Khrushchev's cause was hurt by "insulting remarks" directed at the Central Committee members. Page describes it as "wild, sometimes unashamedly hysterical."

38. Page, p. 100.

▪ Index

Adzhubei, Alexei, 12, 33, 52, 100–101, 127, 190, 196; trip to West Germany (1964), 160–161

Agriculture (USSR), 88, 109, 131, 195; allocations to, see Economic priorities (USSR); animal husbandry, 118–119; Central Committee plenum on (1964), 112–113, 129, 150; commission on intensification of, 118–119; fertilizer, see Chemical industry; grain imports (1963), 116–117, 129; harvest of 1963, 116–118, 125; Khrushchev on, 10, 87, 107, 112, 118–119, 131, 135–136, 138, 180, 196; machine tractor stations (MTS), 15; management reform, 135–136; lagging production, 10, 117, 128–129; party supervision of, 39; payments to farmers, 113, 119

Aksenov, Vasily, 103

Albania, 10, 79

Algeria, 9

Anti-Khrushchev coup (fall 1964)
BY STAGES, formation of coalition, 173–178; early phases, 178–182; Khrushchev's return to Moscow, 197; final phases, 187–197; Suslov's condemnation, 193–196; the resignation, 196–197

ROLE OF CENTRAL COMMITTEE, plenum (Oct. 14, 1964) 197; charges against Khrushchev ("29 Points"), 192, 200n; in removal, 185–186; vote on removal, 196–197

ROLE OF PRESIDIUM, 184–185; meetings, 182–184, 191–192; of key individuals, see Brezhnev, Kosygin, Mikoyan, Podgorny, Suslov

ROLE OF NON-PARTY ORGANS, KGB, 185–186; military, 185–187

Andropov, Yury, 52

Armed forces, USSR, 11, 12, 111;